Singing the Faith

Publications of the Joint Liturgical Group
established in 1963

The Renewal of Worship (1965)
The Calendar and Lectionary (1967)
The Daily Office (1968)
     10th corrected impression (1973)
An Additional Lectionary (1969)
Holy Week Services (1971)
Initiation and Eucharist (1972)
Worship and the Child (1975)
The Daily Office Revised (1978)
Getting the Liturgy Right (1982)
Holy Week Services: Revised and
     expanded edition 1983)
The Word in Season (1988)

Singing the Faith

*Essays by members of the
Joint Liturgical Group on the
use of hymns in liturgy*

edited by

CHARLES ROBERTSON

The Canterbury Press
Norwich

First published 1990 by The Canterbury Press Norwich
(a publishing imprint of Hymns Ancient & Modern Limited)
St Mary's Works, St Mary's Plain,
Norwich, Norfolk, NR3 3BH

British Library Cataloguing in Publication Data
Singing the faith.
1. Catholic church. Public worship. Singing
I. Robertson, Charles
264.0202
ISBN 1-85311-008-6

*Typeset by Advanced Filmsetters (Glasgow) Ltd
Printed and bound in Great Britain by
St Edmundsbury Press Limited
Bury St Edmunds, Suffolk*

Contents

Contents

Members of the
Joint Liturgical Group
1989

The Church of England
The Revd Canon Dr D. C. Gray (Chairman)
The Revd M. R. Vasey

The Church of Scotland
The Revd C. Robertson
The Revd A. Scobie

The Baptist Union of Great Britain and Ireland
The Revd N. Clark
The Revd P. Sheppy

The United Reformed Church
The Revd Dr C. P. Thompson
The Revd J. Wyatt

The Episcopal Church in Scotland
The Revd Dr G. Tellini (Secretary)

The Methodist Church
The Revd Dr G. S. Wakefield

The Roman Catholic Church
The Revd P. M. Gallacher
Dr D. Withey

The Fellowship of the Churches in Christ
The Revd E. G. Greer

The Church in Wales
The Revd D. Thomas

The Presbyterian Church in Wales
The Revd Principal E. ap N. Roberts

During the compilation of this book the Revd C. R. Williamson was a representative of the Church of Scotland, The Revd E. Matthews of the Roman Catholic Church, and the Revd D. MacIlhagga of the United Reformed Church.

The Revd Neville Clark was formerly London Secretary of the Student Christian Movement and Minister at Churches in Kent and Bucks. He is currently Principal of South Wales Baptist College and New Testament Lecturer, University of Wales, Cardiff.

The Revd A. Raymond George was formerly Principal of Wesley College, Headingly, and of Richmond College, Surrey; Tutor of Wesley College, Bristol; President of the Methodist Conference; and Moderator of the Free Church Federal Council. He is the author of *Communion with God in the New Testament* and joint editor of *A History of the Methodist Church in Great Britain*. He is currently Warden of John Wesley's Chapel, Bristol.

The Revd Dr Donald Gray is a Canon of Westminster and Chaplain to the Speaker of the House of Commons. He was President of *Societas Liturgica* 1987–89 and is Chairman of the Alcuin Club. He represents the JLG on the English Language Liturgical Consultations.

The Revd Donald McIlhagga is a Minister of the United Reformed Church presently leading a ministry team in St Ives, Cambridgeshire. He was a former member of the JLG.

The Revd Edward Matthews is a Roman Catholic priest of the Archdiocese of Westminister, who until recently was Secretary to the Liturgy Committees of the Bishops' Conference of England and Wales, and was National Director of liturgical formation.

The Revd Charles Robertson is Minister of Canongate Kirk (the Kirk of Holyroodhouse, Edinburgh) and Secretary to the Panel on Worship of the General Assembly of the Church of Scotland. He was Secretary to the Committees which compiled *Hymns for a Day* and *Songs of God's People*. He is President of the Church Service Society.

The Revd Gianfranco Tellini is Rector of St Mary's, Dunblane, Secretary of the Liturgy Committee of the Scottish Episcopal Church and Lecturer in Theology of Worship at the Faculty of Divinity of Edinburgh University.

The Revd Colin P. Thompson is a Minister of the United Reformed Church and was until recently Chaplain at Sussex University. He is a Lecturer in Spanish Literature at Oxford University and a Fellow of St Catherine's College.

The Revd Gordon S. Wakefield retired from the Principalship of the ecumenical Queen's College at Birmingham in 1987. He has been Recognised Lecturer in Liturgiology at Birmingham University and edited the SCM Press *A Dictionary of Christian Spirituality*, 1983, a subject on which he has done most of his writing. He is a Methodist Minister.

The Revd Colin Williamson is Minister of Aberdalgie and Dupplin, in Perthshire. He was Convener of the Panel on Worship of the General Assembly of the Church of Scotland, and is Secretary to the Church Service Society. He represented the Church of Scotland on the JLG.

1

IN TUNE WITH HEAVEN?

Charles Robertson

Milton's engaging picture of the music makers of heaven is
matched by a prayer for those still living on earth. He
invites us to raise our imagination until we hear the trum-
pets of seraphim and the harps of cherubim accompanying

'those just spirits that wear victorious palms,
Hymns devout and holy psalms
Singing everlastingly.'

We are to respond to this music with the prayer,

'That we on earth, with undiscording voice
May rightly answer that melodious noise—. . .
O may we soon again renew that song
And keep in tune with heaven, till God ere long
To his celestial consort us unite,
To live with him, and sing in endless morn of light!'[1]

To 'keep in tune with heaven' has a significance far beyond
the merely musical, involving as it does the whole of life
lived in harmony with God's will and purpose. But the
reference to music may serve to direct attention to a question that today is steadily coming into sharper focus,
namely, Is the music we use in worship 'in tune with
heaven'? More particularly, are the hymns we sing at worship suited for their purpose, not the least part of which is
to keep us in touch with God and with one another, and to
open doors to fresh and enriching spiritual experiences?

This series of essays by members of the Joint Liturgical
Group may be seen as the beginnings of an answer to these
questions. In the past, the JLG has concerned itself with
matters that are immediately related to the liturgy—for
example, the Calendar and Lectionary, the Daily Office,

Holy Week Services, Worship and the Child, Initiation and the Eucharist. Hymn singing may be seen by some to be not so central nor so fundamental, and it may be thought to be open to question whether it is an appropriate subject for the Group.

Three facts, however, are clear. The first is that for many, hymns are essential to the liturgy and supply the place of liturgical items such as *Gloria in excelsis*, *Kyrie*, *Sanctus*, *Agnus Dei*, and so on. Indeed, as von Allmen suggests, the hymns themselves 'might well be classed among the liturgical attestations of church life, since by them the faithful edify and encourage each other'.[2]

Second, even those churches which are 'traditional' and 'catholic' in their worship are now incorporating hymns as a matter of standard practice into the liturgy, and questions are being raised as to the best way of achieving an appropriate balance between hymns and liturgy.

And third, there has been since the 1960s an unprecedented flow of hymn writing, a great flowering of hymnody. The results have been exciting and expansive, but also perplexing, for the churches have not always known how to assess the value of this unexpected treasure nor how best to use it.

The JLG does not claim to be equipped to answer these questions; nor indeed can it deal with technical questions of literary or musical standards which arise out of the practice of hymn singing. But it is perhaps uniquely placed to gather together some of the liturgical concerns of singing hymns at worship and to set these concerns in a proper liturgical framework. If, as one of our previous publications rather suggested, we have a responsibility for *Getting the Liturgy Right*,[3] can we ignore hymns which for some have always occupied a substantial place in their understanding and practice of the liturgy, and for others are making increasing and on the whole welcome incursions into their liturgical space?

We believe that this work is timely. It was already in preparation some time before the recently established Archbishop's Commission on Church Music, which no doubt will survey the whole field in depth and produce in due course the standard text on the subject. This book is much narrower in its scope—it deals only with hymns and hymn singing as such and not, for example, with wide questions such as the place of music in worship, or the history of hymnody, or the recognition of popular music in all its forms as a legitimate element in worship, or even with more practical matters such as the recruiting and training of choirs and organists, or indeed whether there should be a wider range of agents and instruments in the provision of music for worship.

But for all that the book is restricted, we have sought to place the practice of hymn singing in its own relevant context, and have attempted to relate it to theology, to art and literature, and to use and wont in all our churches. Within the limits of the publication, we have tried to be as helpful as possible, both in terms of the debate to which this book is a short and preliminary contribution and in terms of practical guidance for the choosing of hymns for services and for finding a path through the maze of hymn books currently in use. If a hymn is 'what is uttered in worship, what should be uttered is the glory of the Trinity and the victory of Christ'.[4] If this book supports and strengthens that view, it will have served its purpose.

NOTES

1 Milton, John, *At a Solemn Music.*
2 von Allmen, J.-J., *Worship: Its Theology and Practice* Lutterworth press 1965, p. 169.
3 Jasper, R. C. D. (Editor), *Getting the Liturgy Right* (*Essays by the Joint Liturgical Group on Practical Liturgical Principles for Today*) SPCK 1982.
4 von Allmen, J.-J., *op. cit.* p. 91.

2

WORSHIP AND THEOLOGY

Colin R. Williamson

The essays in this volume deal with a specific aspect of the Church's liturgical life, namely, the place of hymnody in worship. But before such a particular subject can be examined, it is necessary to restate some of those theological premises upon which the discussion is to take place. The temptation to speak of a 'theology of music' should be resisted. Rather, the first principles of theology that lie behind worship should be exposed, so that the activities within worship, such as the singing of hymns, may be seen in true perspective when related to the roots of Christian worship.

Worship is an activity ontologically grounded in the relationships of the Godhead. God has revealed himself as community, in which the Spirit is the Love of the Father towards the Son and the adoration given by the Son to the Father. This movement of love and praise at the heart of God is the power that lies behind creation. We believe that God made all things for his glory and that he made humankind to be the 'priest of creation', expressing for all creation the praise that is the natural response to the creator's love. We are made to be the creature among all creatures who might know the Creator and on behalf of all creatures worship God.

But the failure of man diverted this movement. By the broken communion which resulted from disobedience and rebellion, not only was mankind's approach to God turned aside, but the priestly function for all creation was frustrated. Instead of singing for joy, creation groaned in universal travail awaiting the fulfilment of God's purpose.

This fulfilment was achieved in the Incarnation. Jesus

4

came to be the Priest of creation, to do for us and for all creatures what man fails to do; to offer to God the praise we fail to offer him, and to glorify God in a life of perfect obedience. The coming of Jesus, who is both the Son of God by whom and for whom all things were created and 'bone from our bones, flesh from our flesh',[1] means that at last there is One, clothed in our humanity, who can stand before God for us. He assumes our life, takes on our responsibilities, offers to the Father a life of unbroken communion and obedience, dies our death, rises in our humanity, returns to the Father as the one true Worshipper who now by his Holy Spirit leads us in our worship. As our High Priest, he is the Head of all creation, the Head of the Church, the Leader of the worshipping community, who lives in communion with his Father to intercede for all his creatures. He is, as the writer of the *Epistle to the Hebrews*[2] describes him, the *Leitourgos*, 'a minister in the real sanctuary', the one true Worshipper, the Leader of our worship, who has gone on ahead to lead us in our praise and prayers and intercession.

Christ alone, then, presents the perfect offering of obedience and faithfulness to the Father on our behalf. He is the beloved Son and his self-oblation is accepted as from us. So it is that the primary activity in worship is that of the crucified, risen, ascended, and glorified Lord Jesus Christ, our great High Priest, offering the perfect sacrifice on our behalf and in our name.

The ministry of Christ is directed in two ways. Being of one substance with the Father, he comes to his people as the living Word of God, pardoning, challenging, sustaining, and commissioning them as his Body in Word and Sacrament. His presence in the midst of them is constitutive of the Church. At the same time, Christ bears our humanity and represents us before the Father. His is the offering of faith and devotion which is acceptable to the Father. Our offerings of devotion, dedication, and discipleship, for all that they are presented with sincerity and good intent, cannot be received from us as of right, but only if they be offered in and through Jesus Christ. That they are acknowledged and received is all of grace, for only in Christ are they without blemish.

5

And so we are accepted by God, not because we have offered worthy worship, but because God has provided for us a Worship which is pure and a Worshipper who is true. Our Worship is our joyful *Amen* to Christ's worship: his life is our life, his death is our death, his resurrection is our resurrection, his victory is our victory, his righteousness is our righteousness, his prayers and eternal self-offering to the Father are our prayers and offering to the Father. We are accepted in the Beloved.

Our worship is caught up by the Holy Spirit into that of our High Priest. But not only do we worship with and through Christ; we also and always worship 'with angels and archangels and all the company of heaven' and with the whole Church on earth. This is more than a matter of mere dogma: our service of devotion is joined to what is already happening in heaven and on earth, and it is uplifting and encouraging to recognise that worship is proceeding not only all the time but into all eternity. Indeed, worship is the one activity of the Church which will not cease or be concluded at the *Parousia*.

It is in worship that the Church is most truly herself, the people of God gathered into Christ and thus presented without spot or blemish to the Father. The service of Word and Sacrament is the point to which we are drawn so that empty hands may be filled; and it is the point from which we are sent out, commissioned and equipped for service. It is essentially a point of rest, of being what we are by baptism and calling. Christ, the true Worshipper and the perfect Offering, is all in all, so that in a profound sense our worship should be characterised by an absence of striving and contriving on our part.

This is not to say that we are to assume a passive role in worship or that there is no need carefully to prepare, lead, and participate. But the order and content of worship draw their logic from God's mighty acts of redemption in Jesus Christ. Just as worship is ontologically grounded in the relationships of the Godhead, so the very structure of what we do liturgically has its roots in the Gospel and is evangelically determined. Our worship is a response to the worship and ministry of Christ, and our liturgies ought to set forth what God has done for us and for the world. Our *Public Worship* becomes his *Divine Service* when it is caught up by Christ in the power of the Spirit in such a way that he is the One who acts in and through us, so that our worship becomes real worship in spirit and in truth. We pray and preach and celebrate the sacraments, not to bear witness to ourselves, but to witness to him and to what the world shall become in him. The shape and order of worship, and even its time and place, can never be our sole prerogative to decide: the liberty of the Spirit does not mean that we have license to do as we please. And so it is that the greater part of the Church recognises the inseparable progression of Word and Sacrament as the order for worship dictated by the Gospel itself. Without such an evangelically determined structure, there is a danger of services becoming little more than thematic presentations which are culture-based and man-centred.

Whatever form our worship takes, it should be transparent in setting Christ before the worshipping congregation. Thus, all that we do, for example, in the Christian Year, in Advent, at Christmas, in Lent, at Easter, in Ascensiontide, at Pentecost, at Trinity; all that we do in preaching as well as in Baptism and in Eucharist; all that we do in praying and praising; all should be a sort of *anamnesis*, a setting forth not just the past but the present and future ministry of Christ.

If the nature and the content of our worship are determined by the Gospel, so too are the elements of worship. Worship, for instance, has a social aspect, for individual worshippers are brought into a special relationship with one another, and indeed, worshippers in any one church are brought into fellowship with the whole Church in heaven and on earth. It follows that there must be vehicles to express this communion and to allow it to manifest itself. But since the order of worship is evangelically determined, these vehicles—words, music, movement, gestures, symbolism—must serve the order. Hymns, for example, express the common intent of the worshippers, but they must not be allowed to usurp or supplant the liturgy itself. They help the worshippers to make confession, offer adoration, express hope, or to participate in any of the other elements of worship, all at the appropriate point in the evangelical order of the service. But the liturgy does nor thereby become a mere setting for the hymns: it retains its own logic and integrity as a reflection of and response to the Gospel.

In worship, then, we meet joyfully in the presence of the Risen Lord, to hear the Word of the Cross, to receive forgiveness and renewal, and to be led in our prayers and praises by him who is the true Leader of our worship. Because Christ is 'in the midst', our worship resounds with the 'new song' and unites us with the whole company of the redeemed in heaven and on earth.

NOTES

1   Genesis 2.23.
2   Hebrews 7 & 8, particularly 8.2.

3

SYMBOLS, WORSHIP AND THE WORD

Gianfranco Tellini

'What is truth?', said Pilate to Jesus. Did his words express the cynicism of the experienced politician or the genuine bewilderment of the common man? Nearly two thousand years later, we still await a compelling answer to the question.

The Question of Truth

Is objective knowledge at all possible, or is the picture we have of the world only the construct of the human mind? Should the category of truth be limited to what can be scientifically proven, and all the rest confined to the realm of *personal opinion*? Is it true—as the philosopher A. J. Ayer asserted in a BBC interview not long before his death—that believing in God makes as much sense as believing that there was a rhinoceros in the studio?

The mere fact that some of us still insist in asking this kind of question is ample proof that modern advances in the natural sciences have not yet succeeded in teaching us much about the fundamental limitations of the human mind. Absolute certainty is no more than a dream. As G. B. Vico (1648–1744)[1] explained a long time before the invention of alternative geometries, even the so-called certainty of mathematics depends on premises that, being the invention of the human mind, are ultimately undemonstrable. And, as Nicholas of Cusa (1401–1464)[2] explained even earlier than Vico, the more we truly learn, the more we realise the full extent of our ignorance. The questions multiply. How far does the very mechanism of human perception modify our picture of reality? Is it legitimate to attribute objective existence to what is for ever beyond the direct reach of our senses? Can love, art, or the divine be said to have objective existence? And, more importantly for the topic we wish to discuss, if it can be said that such realities exist beyond the realm of personal opinion, how do we come to know of them and by what means may we try to express them?

The Power of God's Word

To the believer, the objective existence of God is no more of a problem than the objective existence of love to the lover, or of art to the artist. To those who believe, God is as real as anything that may fall under the senses, directly or indirectly. His creative, redeeming and fulfilling power is part of their experience of life: in God they live and move and have their being.

Believing in God is not necessarily a sign of immaturity. We may well try and reach out to a hoped-for God like frightened little children, but it is not we who eventually find him. It is always he who, reaching out to us, finds us first, addresses us personally and endows us with his power to transform both ourselves and the world around us. God speaks, and those who were deaf are made able to hear his call, those who were blind are made able to see his mighty works. The dumb—now able to speak—and the lame—now able to walk—are sent out into the world to proclaim the glories of God's Name.

God's Word may reach us in many and various ways, but always *as in a mirror dimly*, even when the experience of its power has the overwhelming clarity of the vision of Saul on the road to Damascus. It may reach us through a person, a place, or an event. It may reach us anywhere, when we ask for it and when we least expect it. It may reach us through anything that is and anything that happens; but when it does, it is always to confront us with the demand of God's love to go out into the world and be to him a royal kingdom of priests and prophets.

When God gives us a glimpse of his being, his purpose is

not just that of imparting information for us to turn into yet more articles of orthodox belief. God's revelation is ultimately a call to action. It demands active participation in the mystery of his will to bring into a unity in Christ all things in heaven and on earth.[3] Nothing escapes this fundamental rule, not even the activity of worship. The ultimate purpose of the encounter between God and his people is always the bringing to wholeness of all that was made, the fulfilling of his will for the future, the coming of his Kingdom, or in yet different words, the hallowing of his Name.

Worship Pagan and Christian

It is a recognised characteristic of childhood, and therefore of immaturity, to see oneself and one's needs at the centre of the universe. Small infants and very young children firmly believe that all want will be satisfied by manipulating their parents. This childhood trait is nowhere clearer than in the popular conception of worship.

Many cultures, past and present, have chosen to believe that, by accurately performing the appointed ritual, it is possible to reach the gods, influence them, favourably dispose them towards us and eventually cause them to bestow upon us the particular benefits which are the object of our desires. For such cultures, ritual belongs to the realm of the *sacred*: it exists in a world apart, totally cut off from ordinary time and space. Since the prescribed ritual is thought to be the object of divine revelation, its precise form is thought to be both inherently perfect and unchangeable: the appropriate ritual must be performed according to indispensable, absolute and unchangeable rules decreed by the gods themselves. In performing such ritual, the believing community is aware not only of asking for particular benefits, but also of co-operating with the will of the gods who ordained the ritual precisely for that purpose. In less flattering words, it could probably be said that instead of developing a mature personal relationship with a personal God, such worshipping communities behave just like the immature child who has been made aware that, in order to obtain what it wants, it must first learn to say 'please'.

11

Though shared by many a Christian, this primitive understanding of worship is pagan at heart. God's revelation to the Israel of old, the teachings of Jesus and the revelation of the New Testament should have dispelled the magic of this ancient vision, but in practice they have not done so. Nearly two thousand years after Christ, we have not yet succeeded in eradicating altogether from our midst this fundamental misunderstanding. On the contrary, from time to time Christian Churches have even encouraged it. We have often failed to appreciate that worship is not first and foremost something we do, in the presence of God or otherwise, but an encounter between God and his people in which God speaks first, reveals his will, and enables us to respond both in the act of worship and—more to the point—in the everyday life of both the individual and the community of faith.

It is a commonplace of Christian theology to say that, when God speaks, the power of his Word makes a reality of what it says. *A fortiori*, this is also true of when we gather to pray. As the community encounters God again and again through repeated acts of worship, God's Word of power becomes more and more a reality in the lives of the faithful. At work in us, as Scripture says, God's power achieves immeasurably more than all we can ask or conceive:[4] we are made into nothing less than a new creation.[5] As our worship unfolds, our nature is being constantly renewed in the image of the Creator and brought to know God,[6] so that, day by day, both as individuals and as the Body of the Risen Lord, we may grow into a maturity measured by nothing less than the full stature of Christ.[7] When we worship, we are transformed and turned into an instrument of transformation, and so the Church *happens*, because the purpose of the Church, the reason why we worship and the purpose of God for creation are one and the same: the completion of all things in his dear Son.

The Concept of 'Rite'

In technical language, a *rite* is any combination of words and actions used in worship. In this context, the word 'action' should of course be understood to include gestures, movement and postures as well as the use of light, colour, silence and sound. From this point of view, any one individual act of worship can therefore be considered as a *series of rites*. The question now emerging is this: given the understanding of worship we have outlined, what kind of rites should or should not be present in the worship of Christians?

On the face of it, the answer to this question seems easy: worship should contain only those words and actions which express and convey God's call to us, our answer, or both. Encountering God so that we may know and respond to his will in adoration, thanksgiving and obedience is the primary reason why the community gathers to pray. What we say and do must therefore be so directed as to make possible a truly fruitful encounter between God and his people of prophets and priests. Any rite which was not instrumental in reaching this fundamental purpose would at best be irrelevant, and at worst be a positive obstacle to the efficacy of God's Word.

The real difficulty comes when we ask the next question: how are we to know which words and actions are the right ones to use?

The Language of Signs

Human beings possess the ability to evoke the presence of absent realities by means of *signs*. Followers of popular culture may be reminded at this point of Umberto Eco's best-selling novel and of the Latin tag that constitutes its closing line. *Stat rosa pristina nomine: nomina nuda tenemus:* the original rose exists by its name; bare names are what we keep. The rose's former reality is gone; all we possess is *The Name of the Rose*, but when that name (or *sign*) is uttered, the reality to which it refers is made present once more.

Umberto Eco is not just a popular author who happens to have hit the best-sellers list with his very first novel. He is the author of many a scholarly book and article on semiotics. Learned and not-so-learned books on the problem of human communication by means of signs come today in so many shapes and sizes as to make it impossible for us even to begin to comment on the plethora of theories and hypotheses advanced so far by innumerable scholars. On this topic, confusion reigns supreme.

In spite of enormous advances, we still possess too little information about the physiology of the human brain, the mechanisms of of the psyche and the social processes governing the handing-on of the knowledge and experience of our forebears—to mention but three vital areas—for us to be able to speak confidently of the way in which usable signs are invented or found and by what mental mechanisms and cultural rules we are enabled to interpret them. So philosophers are still compelled to make up for the general lack of information by taking for granted a number of unprovable philosophical assumptions.

Theologians often do worse. Though the Bible teaches clearly enough that our nature is that of a single psychophysical unit, some still like to operate on the basis of a Greek-inspired *di*chotomy *soul-body* or even on the basis of a *tri*chotomy *body-soul-spirit*. In the midst of such confusion, a few points should be made clear, not least in order to allow the reader to make up his or her own mind.

The most fundamental of such points regards the nature of human knowledge. As we have already pointed out, no matter how much more we learn, absolute knowledge of the nature of reality will be for ever beyond our reach. What we know is neither the creation of the thinking subject nor the mirror-representation of objective reality, but rather a subjective apperception of the real. In this subjective apperception, the subjective and the objective, the qualitative and the quantitative, the relative and the absolute are aspects of our knowledge that can be distinguished only by means of a phenomenological *reduction* or *suspension* consisting of excluding, or *putting in brackets,* one or more of what we perceive to be equally valid aspects of the real. Human knowledge will always be *relative,* because meaning can only be meaning-for-us.

A second point concerns what may be defined as different *provinces of meaning.* Our conscious life depends on a stream of sensory experience made up by separate and diverse sense impressions which come to us in no particular logical order. As rational beings, we try to make sense both of ourselves and of the world around us by submitting the data of sensory perception to a process of reflection. We need to give meaning to the stream of our sensory experience in spite of its unpredictability and apparent chaotic diversity. We therefore divide such experience into separate compartments which we then explore in isolation the one from the other.

We distinguish between the worlds of wakefulness and dreams, work and play, science and art, and so on. We realise that, in these different sectors of the one stream of experience, we must apply different sets of rules and that, therefore, the different conclusions we reach in these different kinds of areas must have different kinds of validity. Rather than the different *language games* of which L. Wittgenstein speaks,[8] we identify in fact what A. Schutz and T. Luckmann[9] call different *provinces of meaning*. The unity of the hermeneutical process, that is the unity of the process involved in our effort to interpret the data we possess, is safeguarded by the unity of the thinking subject, the unity of the stream of sensory perception and the unity-in-diversity of the language we use to refer to the totality of our knowledge and experience.

In consequence, though partial and relative (in the sense of relative-to-us), our knowledge is nevertheless organic. We could therefore compare it not just to a chain of logical thought suspended between two infinites—as Pascal did— but even more so to a living and growing organism in which all parts are constantly related to each other.

Berger and Luckmann have demonstrated that, in ordinary circumstances, the transition from one province of meaning to another requires a shift of attention the intensity of which is directly proportional to the 'distance' between the province of meaning we leave and the one into which we enter:[10] the shift of attention needed to move from the consideration of a problem in the field of psychology to one in the field of sociology is presumably less than the shift of attention needed to move from the appreciation of a piece of music to a problem of nuclear physics.

We are particularly interested here in three different

sectors of human experience—the world of interpersonal relationships, the world of art and the world of religion: three different areas which are inextricably involved in the experience of worship. The patterns of thought involved in these three provinces of meaning seem to be very similar, if not altogether identical. The rules we apply in all three seem to be the same and so does the kind of validity we are compelled to assign to the conclusions we reach in them. When reflecting in the province of meaning of mathematics or in those of the so-called exact sciences, we *put in brackets* the qualitative aspect of reality and deliberately concentrate on the objectively quantifiable. Exactly the reverse happens in the case of the three provinces of meaning in which we are particularly interested. The conclusions reached at the end of the one type of reflection process are no less *true* than the conclusions reached at the end of the other. They just happen to be true in a different, but equally *valid*, sense.

Let us consider the reality we call *love*. The words and gestures we employ to express it are not in themselves that reality. They can be employed to deceive. Yet, without such outward and visible signs, love is not. Much the same can be said of the reality we call *art*. A well-known painting by Giorgione, *The Tempest*,[11] depicts a town in the distance, a broken column, a guard half-asleep, a wood, a naked woman, a child and a menacing sky. Simply by looking at the painting, we are pushed beyond the level of the objective to a new subjective appreciation of the real. New horizons are opened up to us, because neither the whole work of art nor any one of its elements is in a one-to-one relationship with what Giorgione wishes to express and communicate. His work contains both surplus-meaning and a multiplicity of signification. It affords us a glimpse of the transcendent without ever being able to encompass it altogether. Our thinking and orientation towards life are directed anew. The work of art demands our response and commitment to the reality to which it points, and yet the work of art itself is unequal to all the interpretations it may elicit in the mind of any one viewer at any one time. We could nearly say with the followers of the contemporary French philosopher Paul Ricoeur that a kind of *kerygmatic encounter* takes place between us and the transcendent reality which the painting has the power to evoke and make present.

The third and last point to be made clear is that our whole discourse is based on a general assumption not readily made by all, namely on the belief that there is more to reality than that which our senses can directly perceive. Precisely because we realise that, as we are social beings, our perception of reality must of necessity be a socially constructed one, we would maintain against A. J. Ayer[12] that love, hate, art and the religious are not just a matter of *personal opinion*, but equally valid aspects of the human experience of reality. It is simply not true that only a so-called scientific proof can certify the existence of anything at all. From the days of the Michelson-Morley experiment in 1885 to the positing of the theory of relativity and the discovery of quantum physics, modern scientists have gradually discarded as untenable the old Newtonian view of the universe.[13] A. J. Ayer never did.

As the ancients warned us, whatever is poured in a glass—be it champagne or dishwater—will take the shape of the container and be limited by its capacity. The truth of this dictum should be remembered not just by scientists and philosophers, but by theologians as well. It is not only the language of Christian worship that will be bound by the nature and limitations of the human mind, but even the infinite truth of the self-revelation of the being of God.

It would appear to be a fundamental law of the human condition that only a *special* kind of sign language can make it possible for us to know and express what is real and yet can neither be seen nor completely understood.

A Grammar of Symbols

In common parlance, *symbol* and *sign* are often used as being synonymous. To some, *symbol* may mean no more than an established recognition-sign such as those outside a pawn-broker's or a barber's shop. So a regal figure in a stained-glass window will be easily recognised as King

David by his holding of a harp, the 'symbol' of psalm-writing.

Christian worship is full of symbolism, in whatever way we may care to define it. Even the pointed *absence* of certain symbols is the easily identifiable battle-flag of one's church-manship or denomination.

In worship, *symbol* is often, not unreasonably, a suspect word. For others, it is no more than a familiar, well-worn 'porte-manteau' for a number of different, contradictory meanings. The true nature of symbol is a subject at present too hotly disputed among specialists for us to be able to speak about it with any degree of certainty. Nevertheless, it may prove useful to introduce at this point a provisional distinction between *symbol* and *sign*, providing we see such distinction, for the time being, as no more than a conveni-ent *heuristic hypothesis*.

With T. Fawcett,[14] we might perhaps say that, in general, useful signs have only *one* meaning. They refer to realities which by their very nature are not beyond human compre-hension. According to this view, signs are in a one-to-one, mirror-like relationship to what is signified. Symbols, on the contrary, refer at once, without danger of equivocation, to different things at different levels. They have a multipli-city of signification. As they refer to a reality which is for ever our total grasp, they are in a one-to-many relationship to what is signified. True symbols are only those which, pushing us beyond the level of empirical objectivity, are capable of opening up new horizons to our appreciation of the real whilst never exhausting its ultimate meaning.

According to this kind of terminology, a traffic sign could never be called a *symbol* because a warning indicating dif-ferent things at different times and different levels would be useless. By the same token, the bread and the wine in the Eucharist could not be called *signs* in this sense, both because they are charged at once with multiple, simul-taneous significations, and because they reveal the mystery of Christ without ever exhausting either its meaning or that of the mystery of his presence: in the sacrament of the altar, as the familiar hymn puts it, 'faith believes, nor questions how'.

To establish a sign, we must first agree on a convention. The same is not true of symbols. When Caravaggio painted Christ's disciples with dirty feet, knarled hands and bulging trouser-seats, when Tchaikovsky opened his Sixth Symphony with a slow movement in a minor key, and when Puccini employed a series of consecutive fifths in the opening of the Third Act of *La Bohème*, it was precisely the breaking of the established conventions that gave fresh artistic value to their work. According to Fawcett, no human convention can establish the signifying power of a symbol. No artist can invent, create or imagine it. As every artist knows, symbols are not invented, but *born out of life*. The right word, the desired chord or stretch of melody, the perfect brushstroke, come—in a flash of inspiration—out of the artist's subjective understanding of what life is about.

For this to be true, the link between a symbol and one's experience of life would have to be a very strict one. Moreover, the process of communication of the symbols meaning would also have to have a social dimension, because the symbols a group experiences effectively determine the limits within which that group, be it as large as humankind itself, can understand reality. Symbols are a *social* phenomenon. A change of symbols means a change of the group's view of both self and universe and, conversely, a cultural change in the view of both self and universe demands a change of symbols. In the examples above, Caravaggio, Tchaikovsky and Puccini successfully broke the established conventions precisely because, in their days, society's experience of the real was beginning to change. The change they had been able to perceive was so reflected in their work, that it turned eventually into a powerful instrument for the spreading of the new vision to wider and wider circles. In this, some artists are luckier than others. Not infrequently, part of the price of genius is that one should be so far ahead of the rest of one's fellow-beings as to remain painfully alone. Van Gogh committed suicide in utter poverty and complete despair. It is only today that the value of his work is recognised by all and, needless to say, shamelessly exploited by some.

A culture in which very little changes will favour symbols that imply stability and permanence, but in a rapidly changing world *static* symbols such as *temple, God's house* and *God's eternal throne* will have meaning for but a few. In such circumstances, meaning will more likely be conveyed by *dynamic* symbols implying growth, equality, freedom, stewardship of the earth, fellowship, sharing and the like. Either way, truly viable symbols will be only those that are so deeply rooted in the experience of the society of the time *as to need no explanation at all.*

As the world in which we live changes, so does our perception of it. Accordingly, new symbols will be born and some of the old ones will cease to communicate. Some, but not all. Whilst some symbols are conditioned by, and limited to, the society in which they arise, others are so deeply embedded in the unchanging experience of being human as to be able to transcend space and time. So the sharing of one's food is likely to be recognised by peoples of all times and cultures as a token of friendliness and goodwill, when the shaking of a Maori spear, accompanied by deliberately mocking and frightening noises, is unlikely to fill with confidence anyone unfamiliar with that welcoming custom. Temporally and spatially conditioned, symbols will—theoretically—live and die, but some, more universal ones will at worst become dormant and remain so only until our sensitivity to them is attuned once more.

How and when do symbols work? Backed at once by recent discoveries in psychology, psychoanalysis, social anthropology and in the physiology of the human brain, the contemporary philosopher Paul Ricoeur argues throughout his work that for a symbol to *communicate* successfully the following three conditions must apply at one and the same time:

(1) the social group within the confines of which the symbol is to operate must have the experience of the literal meaning of the symbolic form of expression being employed;

(2) the group must also have at least a rudimentary experience of the reality towards which the symbol is pointing;

(3) lastly, both the literal and the symbolic meaning of the

mode of expression used must be associated with each other in a way so rooted in the common experience of that group, as to be perceivable by, and acceptable to, most of its members.

For example, Ricoeur asks, in what circumstances will we be able to communicate meaning by saying that 'sin' is a 'stain'? In the first place, the statement will be understood only by a society in which cleanliness is a virtue. The statement would make little sense in a society in which personal uncleanliness caused neither guilt nor embarrassment. In the second place, the statement would work only in a society whose members have experienced, however rudimentarily, the guilt and shame of alienation from God. The statement would make no sense at all in a society that had no awareness of sin. Yet the common social experience of both the literal and the symbolic meaning of a statement is not enough for the symbol to communicate successfully.

The third condition postulated by Ricoeur must also apply. After the customary Confession and Absolution, a Christian congregation of the 1960s attempted to symbolise God's forgiveness by the individual pulling of the lavatory chain in the vestry's toilet. The literal meaning of that action is not unknown. The most hardened of sinners among us has at least a rudimentary awareness of the shamefulness of one's sin. Yet, not many of us would dream of associating the two experiences in an act of worship for the purpose of conveying meaning. The congregation in question is reported to have found in the ceremony great significance and effectiveness, but most of us would find it outrageously inappropriate and screamingly funny.

When the delicate balance of the three pre-conditions postulated by Paul Ricoeur is broken, the symbol dies, or— when deeply rooted in our psyche—it becomes dormant until the required balance is re-established. In such cases, the symbol ceases to point to the transcendent. It demands commitment only to itself. We are then confronted with a particularly insidious kind of idolatry. However unwittingly, the community ends by worshipping not God but the symbol, itself, or both. Such symbols have ceased to exist in and for the encounter which is worship. Whatever they may convey, it is not the power of God's Word. As a result, our worship is pushed out of life into a realm of its own. It becomes pagan rather than Christian: a sequence of spells and incantations effectively preventing the growth of the congregation into a more mature relationship with God. In the worst cases, the dead or dormant symbols take on a demonic life of their own and, with frightening precision, effectively point the unsuspecting congregation away from both God and his will.

It is at this point that, as it did towards the end of the Middle Ages, the impulse towards liturgical reform becomes overwhelming. Hurried surgical interventions are then performed on the living tissue of the Church's prayer, in spite of the fact that, in real life, such operations have often been known to lead to the death of the patient.

To avoid this danger, the liturgical reformer could do well to remember that in Christian worship not all things are open to negotiation. Throughout the ages, God remains the same. So do his grace, his love and his purpose towards us. An encounter and dialogue with the God of unchanging graciousness and power, the nature of Christian worship will therefore also remain the same even though we may fail to recognise some of its major aspects for long periods of time. Neither will the fundamental constituent elements of any particular service ever change. There will never be a Service of the Word without some reading of the Scriptures. There will never be a baptism without washing, or a Eucharist without food and drink. Such constituent elements of the different types of services are given, once and for all. They are inherent to the inner structure of the service itself, and not open to negotiations.

At the same time, the conservative ones among us could also do well to remember that, if neither God nor the nature of worship can possibly change, we change, and so do also the world around us, our self-understanding and our experience of life. For this reason, and for this reason alone, no one of our worship formularies will be so perfect in every detail as to be capable of being used in perpetuity with no change in wording, music and ceremonial by peoples of all times and cultures. Pretending that such a perfect, unchanging worship formulary can exist would be as foolish as trying to reach out to the absolute in an attempt to exhaust its meaning.

The Function of Liturgical Symbols

Human nature demands that the search for suitable liturgical symbols should go beyond the search for mere words. By itself, fine speech may lack the power to convince. Left to themselves, actions and gestures may lead to equivocation. It is only when they are appropriately linked together that words, actions and gestures may reach the summit of the power to communicate.

According to the Belgian psychologist and sociologist Antoine Vergote,[15] human activity may be broadly divided into two categories: technical and symbolic.

A technical action, such as the driving of a nail into a wall in order to hang a picture, does not communicate at the level of the personal. It achieves a pre-determined end through the manipulation of tools. Symbolic actions, such as a kiss or an embrace, will on the contrary express an intention and, while expressing it, achieve it at the same time. Technical actions demand no personal commitment, but symbolic actions express, achieve and demand commitment to the *other*. Such actions exist in and for an encounter. No tools can achieve such end. Therefore symbolic actions involve no manipulation of any kind. Should there be such manipulation, the action would cease to be symbolic. It would revert to the state of a technical action, a means to an end. It is for this reason that no magic quality can be attributed to a rite, be it even a sacramental one. What a rite symbolises cannot be sought as an end to itself apart from the encounter in which and for which the rite operates.

Symbolic actions achieve what they signify simply by expressing an intention. It is through symbols that God calls; it is through symbols that God empowers; and it is through symbols that we respond. Vergote so concludes:

'to say that liturgical gestures are a system of symbols implies

23

also that they achieve of themselves life with God. They *are* life with God, the action of faith that is accomplished. They have no finality outside that which they achieve. And to ordain a finality with them is to destroy their symbolic efficacy'.[16]

In other words, the *right* liturgical words and gestures possess no pre-determined human finality. They are not tools open to manipulation. A rite performs its function only when it becomes the instrument of the power of God's Word.

Devising an Act of Worship

Devising an act of worship is not a matter of personal preference. Neither is it a matter for amateurs. It needs a number of professional skills. It asks for a high degree of professional integrity. Above all, it demands great sensitivity. In this sense, devising a service is a highly skilled labour of love that can be compared only with the work of an artist.

Before one can even begin to devise an act of worship, there are three basic requirements. The first and most obvious one is the experience that comes from a deep and personal commitment to a life of prayer. Only those who know how to pray can lead others in that kind of exercise. The second is an adequate theological understanding of the nature and purpose of Christian worship and the awareness of what cultural forces and popular expectations may tend to pervert them. The third and last is an understanding of the nature of the service and of those elements of it which are not subject to change or open to negotiations.

After this, the devising of a service becomes a matter of sensitivity. Words alone will not suffice. To perceive the transcendent reality of God and to respond to his call, we need to choose from the full range of symbolic expression.

Symbols may be verbal as in poetry, or non-verbal as in music, dance, architecture and the representational arts: to encounter God in worship to the best of our ability we must employ them all. We need words, actions and gestures, movement, light, colour, music and silence.

Yet a plethora of symbols is not always synonymous with

increased communication. We must not underestimate the value of the calculated silence of the *absence* of symbols. We need to be able to discern which symbols are still operative in our group, which are dormant, and which are dead. Dead symbols should be discarded. Dormant symbols could, and sometimes should, be revived with the help of teaching and gentle persuasion. The symbols we use must not only be meaningful in themselves. In order to communicate successfully, they must also be capable of being understood by the worshipping community at large.

In this respect, the quality of the symbols used will depend largely on the cultural conditions of the time and on the particular sub-culture to which the worshipping community belongs. It may be foolish to try and introduce guitar music or a revival song to the congregation of an English cathedral on the grounds that it appears to be working with a young congregation in a Mission Hall. In the same way, dance and some forms of the representational arts may not immediately recommend themselves to our native culture. However, as the history of Christian worship shows, we would be foolish if we did not attempt to harness to our purpose the power of silence and sound. No human culture has been immune to the fascination of music, except perhaps that of the Dayaks of Borneo, who—in recent times—were nevertheless remorselessly introduced to the delights of *The English Hymnal*.

Almost universally, music can be a powerful symbol indeed. When carefully chosen, and placed at the right point in the service, instrumental music may move us more than any number of well thought-out words. On its own, music can create and sustain a condition of openness to God and also underline the meaning of what has been said and done so far in the service. Combined with the words of a hymn or a song, it can open up new horizons and dimensions of understanding, and thereby help us to elicit the necessary unqualified commitment to the demands of God's grace.

Beyond this point, there are no rules. Whatever achieves the purpose should be used, and whatever does not should be discarded. Antoine Vergote warns us that the worship of

God's people should be imaginative and daring. It should open up new ways of understanding our faith, our commitment and the Church's place and mission in the world. It should be at once challenging, comforting and disturbing. Above all, it should provide an answer to the many needs of our times and speak to us—in utter simplicity—in our native idiom. In his own words, 'it is not only by reassessing the ethical demands of Christianity that we can overcome the dreaded rift between worship and life, but by assuming into the rite all that is human in civilisation'.[17]

NOTES

1   Vico, G. B., *La Scienza Nuova*, 3rd ed., Axiom 1 (1744).

2   Nicholas Chrypffs of Cusa, *De Docta Ignorantia* (1440).

3   *Eph. 1*, 10.

4   *Eph. 3*, 20.

5   *Gal. 6*, 15.

6   *Col. 3*, 10.

7   *Eph. 4*, 13.

8   Wittgenstein L., *Philosophical Investigations*, Oxford 1968.

9   Schutz, A. and Luckmann T., *The Structures of the Life-World*, London 1974.

10 Berger, P. and Luckmann, T., *The Social Construction of Reality: A Treatise on the Sociology of Knowledge*, London 1973, p. 35.

11 The painting is displayed in the Accademia of Venice and a black-and-white reproduction of it can be seen on p. 115 of Kenneth Clark's *Civilisation*, London 1979.

12 Ayer, A. J., *Language, Truth and Logic*, London 1936.

13 *Cf.* e.g. Heisenberg, W., *Physics and Philosophy*, London 1959.

14 Fawcett, T., *The Symbolic Language of Religion: An Introductory Study*, London 1970, pp. 13–37.

15 Vergote, A., *Symbolic Actions and Gestures in the Liturgy*, in: *Concilium*, vol. 2, February 1971, pp. 40–52.

16 *Ibidem*, p. 52.

17 *Ibidem*, p. 45.

FURTHER READING

Greeley, A., *Religious Symbolism, Liturgy and Community*, in: *Concilium*, vol. 2, n. 7, February 1971, pp. 59–69.

Rasmussen, D., *Mythic-Symbolic Language and Philosophical Anthropology*, Nijhoff 1971.

Ricoeur, P., *Fallible Man*, Chicago 1965; *Freud and Philosophy: An Essay in Interpretation*, Newhaven-London 1970; *The Rule Of Metaphor: Multi-disciplinary Studies of the Creation of Meaning in Language*, London 1978.

4

ART IN CHRISTIAN WORSHIP

Colin P. Thompson

God, the only true Artist, created the heavens and earth out of nothing. His art continues to delight and to awe us and we experience it in many forms—the fresh green foliage and birdsong of a May morning in England, the splendour of the night sky deep in the countryside, the joy and intimacy of human love. From the tiniest forms of life to the stars and galaxies in the vastness of space the whole creation is his work of art and shows forth his majesty:

'The heavens tell out the glory of God,
Heaven's vault makes known his handiwork.'[1]

Within it men and women have a special place, for they alone are created in the image of God[2] and given responsibility over the rest of creation.[3] God did not create men and women only that they should manifest his wisdom and glory, but that they should worship him and participate in the divine life.

Music has become a symbol of the harmony of God's created order, in which each element plays its own appointed tune. In his great poem of divine and human love, the *Cantico espiritual* (*Spiritual Canticle*), St John of the Cross hymns the *musica callada*, or *silent music*, of the Beloved. He was no doubt thinking of the verses of the same psalm:

'One day speaks to another,
night to night imparts knowledge,
and this without speech or language
or sound of any voice.
Their sign shines forth on all the earth,
this message to the ends of the world.'[4]

The music we offer in worship, with words or without them, enables us to respond with voice and tongue to the silent but eloquent glory of God.

The ancient stories at the beginning of the Bible tell how God's work of art was tarnished by human disobedience. Into the world of harmonious relationships come shame and exile, death and murder, corruption and violence, and division.[5] They all undermine and tend to destroy what God has made good, and they do so with the seductive promises of power and knowledge independent of any moral constraint or sense of responsibility. These stories, when sensitively understood, remain telling commentaries on our own experience. The same green countryside is plundered and polluted; terrible weapons track through space and threaten us with annihilation; those same human relationships turn sour with envy, betrayal and abuse. Our power and our knowledge are great, greater than in any previous generation; yet we still do not know how to cope with them and their consequences and too often we find that what we have made turns against us and menaces us.

We might say that our world is like a beautiful painting, damaged but not altogether destroyed by centuries of grime and neglect. We have become so used to seeing it in this condition and still regarding it as fine, that we imagine it must always have been like this and always will be. Yet its colours were once bright and fresh; and though it has become so obscured that it takes vision and faith to re-imagine the original and painstaking skill to clean it, it is not beyond restoration. For Christians, the highest expression of the artistry of God is seen in a life which is so fully human that we know it is our life, and so fully divine that it reveals both the cause of the grime and neglect and the splendour of the original. The life of Christ among us calls us to practise the art of restoration in ourselves and our societies, and brings us the gifts to carry it out.

Jewish and Christian traditions, in different ways, have always wanted to distinguish between art which arises out of our fallenness and expresses our alienation from God, and art which seeks to be an image of goodness, beauty and truth and to point us towards God. Art in this fallen world

is therefore bound to be ambivalent, and that helps us to
understand why our religious traditions contain so many
contrasting attitudes towards its place in worship. Art can
be debased into propaganda or be cheapened into the kind
of advertising which arouses only a desire to possess; it can
beget error and pander to ignorance and greed. The image
can become an idol, feeding on superstitition and fear, replacing God with the glorification of man or the state. The
art of totalitarian regimes of the right and left is the clearest
example. Shelley's Ozymandias witnesses to the pretensions
and the illusions of such art:

'My name is Ozymandias, king of kings,
Look on my works, ye mighty and despair!'

For such reasons there has been a long history of icono-
clasm in Christianity, and it is by no means confined to Prot-
estantism. The iconoclastic controversy was conducted
with fierce passions in the eighth century, long before the
Reformation.

It has often been said that human beings are creative
because they are made in the image of the Creator. From
prehistoric times our ancestors have taken the raw mater-
ials of creation, have worked on them and re-ordered them
to make tools and weapons and to provide food, shelter,
clothing and goods for trading. The monuments to their
sense of the mystery of existence remain as silent testimo-
nies to long-vanished faiths and gods. Before ever there was
writing, there were scenes of men and animals and hunting
painted on the walls of caves. Still the pyramids of Egypt,
the temples of the Maya, the great circle of Stonehenge,
astonish us and sometimes disturb us. In the little that we
understand of them we recognise part of that long search
after God which has made such marvels and sanctified so
much bloodshed.

Yet the ambivalence of art in a fallen world should not
blind us to its potential. We do not say that discipleship is
impossible because our sinfulness impedes it, and no more
should we say that art is unredeemable because it has been
corrupted into idolatry. Art, inspired by the Creator and
offered in prayer and humility, can become a sign which

opens us out through colour, shape and sound to all that God has done in freeing us from the burden of sin and healing our brokenness. As such, it can be a window through which we glimpse something of his glory and of the liberty and splendour of the children of God, for which he has destined his own. It can act as a catalyst, enabling change and development to take place in our spiritual growth.

Art here is being defined in its broadest sense. It is not the subject as it appears on the school timetable, nor is it art in the narrower meaning of painting, carving and sculpture. *Art* means the many and varied forms in which human beings express what is most precious to them: it is not simply particular techniques. It is representational and non-representational, concrete and abstract; it includes art which creates figures and scenes which represent the visible world, so that we can see as with new eyes into the ordinary and the mundane; and equally, art weaves patterns out of words and sounds and movement, like poetry, music and dance. It can even be a way of talking about human life when as with the saints, life is so ordered and composed that God becomes more real to us through it. Art, in sum, is a metaphor for all human creativity, and religious art a metaphor for all our response in worship, service and mission to the supreme, self-giving Creator.

How can religion, how can the ultimate mystery of God, be expressed through such common things as water, wood and stone? In such a question there are shades of a Platonic unease, still felt by many faithful Christians: God and physical matter are incompatible. Matter is changing, corrupt and perishable; God is changeless, pure spirit, immortal. To use physical matter as a means of reaching out to God is surely to run the risk of pantheism or idolatry. Yet Christianity, deeply influenced as it was by Plato, rejected such opinions when it affirmed the Incarnation. God himself chose the way of involvement with the fallen creation when he reached out to redeem us from our sin. In choosing to become incarnate in order to reveal himself most perfectly, he committed himself to the world of matter and of sense. Writing in the eighth century from his monastery of Mar Sabbas in the Judean wilderness, in the first of his classic apologies against the iconoclasts, St John of Damascus (himself a great hymn writer) elaborated his Christian theology of art:

'In former times God, who is without form or body, could never be depicted. But now when God is seen in the flesh conversing with men, I make an image of the God whom I see. I do not worship matter; I worship the Creator of matter who became matter for my sake, who willed to take His abode in matter; who worked out my salvation through matter. Never will I cease honouring the matter which wrought my salvation. I honour it, but not as God's.[6]

The life of Jesus Christ, the places and people he moved among, the things he said and did, the stories he told, the suffering and death he endured, count. Because they count, our own lives with all their particularities count. They count so much that this same Christ who was put to death rose from the dead and ascended to the Father on high to show us that the eternal and the spiritual are present in the transient and the material and that while we live on earth we may have the foretaste of the joys of heaven. That is why the symbols of this revelation—the manger and the Cross; the water, bread and wine; Galilee, Jordan, Jerusalem, Golgotha—are preserved in Christian devotion, and live in Christian worship. They do not devalue the symbols of our own age and the times and places in which we live; rather they are present in them and illuminate them. That too is why we remember the names and lives of all kinds of people, in the Bible and in the history of the Church. They do not diminish us and our names and lives or detract from our worship of God; rather they accompany us and inspire us, especially when, as so often, we are tempted to abandon our own poor attempts at discipleship.

All Christian worship is art, art called forth by the Artist, art which longs to glorify him and which creates images through which our capacity for worship is awakened and nourished. The words and music of our hymns are art every bit as much as statues and vestments and incense. We use our bodies and our senses as vehicles for our worship whatever Christian tradition we come from. Our *plainest* wor-

32

ship is as man-made as our most elaborate ceremonial, and necessarily so, because God wants us to worship him as human beings, not as disembodied spirits. It is just as easy to make idols of words, customs and hymn tunes as it is of plaster saints!

The art of Christian worship reasserts divine sovereignty over all that God has made; 'everything comes from you, and it is only of your gifts that we give to you.'[7] It reclaims for him what humans have taken for themselves and idolised. There is more danger in our western culture today that we give our worship to human creations and especially to possessions, status and the cult of personalities, than that we will mistake the signs and images we use in our worship for the One towards whom they point. That may be why suspicion of representational religious art has been decreasing in some Protestant circles which banished it from their churches. It is the golden calf we need to resist,[8] not the bronze serpent;[9] the making of our own gods, rather than the image on which to look is life.

Some examples may be of help. In Coventry Cathedral there is a cross made out of twisted nails found in the ruins of the old cathedral after it had been destroyed by bombs in the Second World War. War is a scourge and shatters the faith of many people. They can no longer see God for all the cruelty and terror and it is not hard to understand why. Those nails remind the Christian of the nails which fastened Christ to the Cross, and their twisting recalls the torturing of his body on the Cross they represent. That too was an experience of darkness and despair, and those who had put their hope in him fled from the sight. But the cross of nails was also born out of the agony of our own century; and though it was forged in the bombing and the firestorm, it does not speak of the futility of all human ideals and all human striving after peace. It speaks of beauty out of ashes, of hope stronger than death, of the resurrection of love. Its voice is not a refuge from the bitter realities of war, for it is uttered in their very midst and has arisen out of their very ruins.

The great artists of our own time may not always be orthodox Christians and the unfamiliar techniques they use can seem so beyond our reach that we are tempted to dismiss them. But they often have a deep spiritual awareness and the gift of communicating it in a new and startling fashion. In terms of words and music there can be few twentieth-century works of art as powerful as Benjamin Britten's *War Requiem*. In it Britten boldly set alongside the traditional Latin text of the requiem mass for the dead several poems by Wilfred Owen, who was himself killed in action during the last few days of the Great War. In that war, as much as in the Second, confidence in a European civilisation built on Christian values was overwhelmed in the mud and slaughter. The chorus sings the liturgical text, while the tenor soloist becomes the twentieth-century commentator on it through the words of Owen, whose subject was war and the pity of war.

At one point the requiem text refers to God's promise to 'Abraham and his seed for ever'. Alongside this, Britten sets Owen's grim retelling of the story of Abraham's sacrifice of Isaac, in whom that promise rested. Owen writes from a place where hundreds of thousands of young men have been killed. The old man refuses to slay the ram caught in the thicket in place of his son, as the angel commands:

'But the old man would not so, and slew his son,
And half the seed of Europe, one by one.'

'And one by one, and one by one' the soloist repeats, several times, between silences, urgently insisting on the horror, the blasphemy of what has happened. God's promise of fruitfulness and life is denied when man follows his own sinful instincts and will not listen to the divine command. Britten the artist joins contemporary experience and ancient liturgy and makes the connection between liturgy and life which so often eludes us.

In the same work, as the chorus softly sings *Agnus Dei* 'O Lamb of God, that takest away the sin of the world, have mercy upon us,' the soloist sings of 'One who ever hangs where shelled roads part'. Owen pictures a crucifix he has seen at a crossroads in a place damaged by shelling. The figure on the crucifix is also maimed: 'In this war he too lost a limb.' So the 'gentle Christ' continues to be denied by the beast[10] masquerading as patriotism and demanding allegiance to the state:

'But they who love the greater Love
Lay down their life: they do not hate'

So as the bread of Eucharist is broken and the body and blood of Christ is given to be shared among his people for their healing, the Lamb 'slain from the foundation of the world'[11] lays down his life to show us our folly and his better way. Juxtaposing these two texts, Britten's music allows Owen to interpret the Eucharist, and the Requiem to interpret war. Neither text is violated; both are enriched.

Christian worship draws on a treasury of biblical images and a long artistic heritage, and both the preacher and the artist who make those images live are called to open their hearts and minds to a great love for God. In worship we look forward to a world redeemed from sin and death and we celebrate the birth of that new world among us in Christ and its growth among us in the life of the Church. Our worship is therefore so to be ordered that in its every part it looks towards God. Though it connects with our everyday life in the sense that it guides and inspires it, it is a mistake to think that it must be like our everyday life in its ordering, full of the familiar and the trivial. In worship God comes to us to disturb our ease and summon us to discipleship. The art of worship helps us to remember that and to fix it in our hearts and minds. Its words will not always be everyday words, thoughtlessly chosen, loosely used. The building in which it is offered will not be like a home or office or school. Our actions and gestures will not be those in the supermarket or at a party. In worship all art becomes icon—the art of movement, an icon of God's moving among us; the art of building, an icon of the household of faith and the city of God; the art of words, an icon of the Word made flesh. No icon exists for its own sake or to bring glory to its begetter. Every icon is like a gateway through which we pass into a closer communion with God.

We are commanded to love God with all our heart, with all our soul, with all our strength, with all our mind.[12] The commandment suggests a wholeness of loving, a uniting of all our faculties out of their customary separation. It is therefore right that our worship should involve our bodies, minds and spirits and express a harmony of intellect and emotion. The joining of words and music in the singing of God's praises is an art which involves at least three of our senses, hearing, sight and touch, and it is a complex one. It reaches far back into the Hebrew Scriptures, and especially the Psalms; it was familiar to Jesus and his disciples[13] and commended by Paul.[14] Those traditions which have come from a reaction against over-elaborate forms of art in worship—and in British terms that means the Reformed and Protestant Churches—may be relatively plain in church ornamentation and ritual, but they have a great richness in their hymnody. Hymns are at the heart of the best nonconformist liturgy and are integral to it, not decorative pieces or gap-fillers. They encourage devotion, they are the vehicle for the people's active participation and they teach through art the truths of the Christian faith.

When the reformers took the images from the walls they often put them into words, so that the people could internalise their meaning. The imagery of many hymns is surely the verbal equivalent of the great reredos or frescoes of the Middle Ages. Is it not a crucifix Isaac Watts draws so movingly, and does he not want us to respond to it through the art of poetry?

> 'See from his head, his hands and feet
> Sorrow and love flow mingled down.
> Did e'er such love and sorrow meet?
> Or thorns compose so rich a crown?'

And he gives us an icon of the saints as bright as a stained-glass window when he prays:

> 'Give me the wings of faith to rise
> Within the veil, and see
> The saints above, how great their joys
> How bright their glories be!'

Charles Wesley's picture of the ascended lord bearing his wounds in triumph breathes a spirit of mystical fervour normally associated with Roman Catholic spirituality:

'The dear tokens of this passion
Still His dazzling body bears;
Cause of endless exultation
To his ransomed worshippers.
With what rapture
Gaze we on those glorious scars!'

Christian hymnody is an ecumenical art, and is therefore
an appropriate subject for the Joint Liturgical Group. We
have used each other's words and sung each other's music
for a long time. It is one of the best ways of entering into
one another's spiritual inheritance as pilgrims, of making
that inheritance our own, and growing thereby in faith and
unity. For, like all Christian art, it comes from the same
source and seeks the same end. In a psalm which has given
us one of our greatest hymns, 'Glorious things of thee are
spoken', an unknown poet wrote of the holy mount of
Zion, chosen and loved by God;

'Singers and dancers alike say
All my springs are in you'.[15]

The spring of all Christian art is the mystery of God the
Holy Trinity and the revelation of the Son in human shape
and form. That makes it quite different from art which
exalts a human patron or the power of the state, however
magnificent it be. It is a way of testifying to the truth which
our ears and eyes and hands have received:

'It was there from the beginning; we have heard it; we have seen
it with our own eyes; we looked upon it, and felt it with our
own hands: one theme is the Word which gives life . . . made
visible to us . . . we declare to you also.'[16]

Christian art begins with the love of God, which renews
our imagination and vision, and it responds to his glory
through that renewal. It cannot but express itself, even
though that expression be but a stammering, a shadow of
the original. It continues with commitment, craftsmanship
and devotion, all of which involve hard work and long
hours, so that the spirit of the divine may more and more
breathe through what is being made. As we sing our hymns,
participate in our liturgies, and contemplate our icons, we

are inspired to possess within us what is represented as outside us. God the Holy Spirit opens our eyes and our hearts to the glories of divine love. None of this is for its own sake, but so that our discipleship shall be the more joyful and the more complete. For the greatest work of art any of us can bring into the presence of God is a life which abides in Christ, the icon of the Father given for a fallen world, in whom matter and spirit, art and the Artist, are at one.

NOTES

1   Psalms 19.1. The Revised English Bible, Oxford University Press, Cambridge University Press, 1989.

2   Genesis 1.27.

3   Genesis 1.28; 2.20.

4   Psalms 19.2–4. The Revised English Bible, *op. cit.*

5   Genesis 3.1–11; 9.

6   St John of Damascus, *On the Divine Images* trans by David Anderson (Gestwood, N.Y.: St Vladimir's Seminary Press 1980), p. 23.

7   1 Chronicles 29.14. The Revised English Bible, *op. cit.*

8   Exodus 32.

9   Numbers 21.6–9.

10   Revelation 13–18.

11   Revelation 13.8.

12   St Luke 10.27.

13   St Mark 14.26.

14   Colossians 3.16.

15   Psalms 87.7. Revised Standard Version. Thomas Nelson & Sons, 1952.

16   1 John 1.1–3. The Revised English Bible, *op. cit.*

5

THE WORD AND MUSIC

Charles Robertson

Christian discipleship embraces the whole of life, including that part of it which is consciously given over to corporate acts of worship. No Christian community is free to do what it likes in terms of worship. For one thing, there are certain acts which, as faithful disciples, Christians must always do or allow to be done: the people must come together in Christ's name so that he may be in their midst;[1] the Word of God must be preached;[2] and the Lord's Supper must be celebrated.[3] The gathering, the preaching, the celebrating, these are mandatory and must not be omitted. Everything else that happens in worship is voluntary, but nothing must obscure or diminish the basic requirements of worship. Nor does *voluntary* mean that activities may be chosen merely at the whim of the worshippers, or be directed by their prejudices and predilections. For here, too, the principle of discipleship, of loving obedience, operates. The freedom we have in worship is the freedom given to those who have heard the Word of God through the Holy Spirit. It is a freedom to serve the Lord of the Church.

St Paul enunciates this principle when he says, 'Let the message of Christ dwell among you in all its richness'.[4] It is significant that he goes on to point up a connection between 'instructing and admonishing each other with the utmost wisdom' and 'singing thankfully in your hearts to God, with psalms and hymns and spiritual songs'. Whatever these three categories of singing precisely comprised, it is evident that they are here given a specific function. Singing is both a proclamation and a witness, an occasion of teaching and instruction, an activity inspired by the Holy Spirit which itself becomes the instrument of further inspiration. The idea that singing has a definite function is reinforced in St Paul's commentary on worship: 'I will sing hymns with my spirit, but with my mind as well . . . when you meet for worship, each of you contributing a hymn, some instruction, a revelation, an ecstatic utterance, or its interpretation, see that all of these aim to build up the church.'[5] Singing has a real job of work to do, a job which, in St Paul's terms, is not far removed from C. S. Lewis's dictum that 'nothing should be done or sung or said in church which does not aim directly or indirectly at glorifying God or edifying the people or both'.[6]

But why sing at all? After all, in that same Essay,[7] Lewis argues that church music is unpleasant, unhelpful, and may even be harmful, and singing hymns, in particular, is nothing more than *shouting*.[8] He found little in it to suggest that God might be glorified and the people edified by it. But, as Erik Routley has pointed out, it is in the nature of things that people should want to sing, and the Bible makes provision for man's response to this natural law.[9] The Old Testament characteristically enjoins the people to 'Sing to the Lord'.[10] The New Testament is sparse in references to singing but it is clear that the Christian Church was a singing Church. The Church immediately after Pentecost 'praised God and enjoyed the favour of the whole people';[11] and St James answers his own question. 'Is anyone in good heart?' with the cheerful reply, 'Let him sing praises'.[12] St Paul encourages the Christians at Ephesus to 'Speak to one another in psalms, hymns, and songs', and adds, 'sing and make music from your heart to the Lord.'[13] The reason for all this singing, whether in the Old Testament or the New, is always the same: it is in response to God for his goodness. In particular, Christians sing in response to God's gift in Christ. Indeed, the writer of the *Letter to the Hebrews* insists that Christ himself sings with them for he is the Son who 'does not shrink from calling men his brothers, when he says, I will make your fame known to my brothers; in the midst of the assembly I will praise you'.[14] This surely is a wonderful picture: Christ and all his brethren singing together the praise of his Father and of their Father in the one act of worship and proclamation.

Here we reach the heart of the matter. The Church of the New Testament sings in the presence of the Word, in response to the Word, and to express the Word. All her music making is related to the function of serving the present Word. In practice, this means that the words we sing must express the Word, and the music we use to sing them must convey the message of the Word. As Erik Routley remarks, 'our music and our music making must aim at being conformable to a gospel which tells of a crucified and risen Redeemer, and which lays on us all the duty and the delight of losing our lives that we may save them'.[15] Father Joseph Gelineau S. J., from a quite different tradition, makes a similar point when he writes, 'As an integral, though not necessary element in Christian worship, music, like all the arts, is dependent on the sacred action whose meaning it is intended to enrich. And when music is vocal, it is dependent, in particular, on the ritual words of which it is the vehicle. . . . Serving the rite humbly and nobly entails serious consequences for music. . . . One single principle emerges, the music of worship is functional.'[16]

Once it be accepted that music is functional, and that its function is to make eloquent among us the present Word, the consequences, as Gelineau suggests are serious, and some of them are intensely practical. For example, does it serve the Word better to sing in unison or in parts? Dietrich Bonhoeffer is in no doubt that unison singing is a better expression of the Word than part-singing:

> 'Because it is bound wholly to the Word, the singing of the congregation, especially of the family congregation, is essentially singing in unison. Here words and music combine in a unique way. . . . The purity of unison singing, unaffected by alien motives of musical techniques, the clarity, unspoiled by the attempt to give musical art an autonomy of its own apart from the words, the simplicity and frugality, the humaneness and warmth of this way of singing is the essence of all congregational singing.'[17]

Many people would not agree with this position, for clearly, some music is written in a unison texture, and much is not. But objections to unison singing, on other than strictly musical grounds, must be theological rather than

41

temperamental if they are to be sustainable. If it be claimed, for example, that singing in unison does not allow the singers to use their best notes, either because the melody rises too high for the men or falls too low for the women; or if it be suggested that unison singing, from the point of view of the singers, is not so interesting as part-singing; the question has to be asked: What is the function of the singing—is it to please the singers, or to express the Word?

Again, what about music which tends to inhibit the growth of the people of God, both as individuals and as a Christian community? Does the exclusive use of the gospel-song tradition of music, for instance, achieve anything other than a restriction of the believer's faith within a very narrow compass? An exclusive use of any other kind of music, whether it be plainsong, German chorales, Genevan psalms, or folk music would need to be similarly questioned. The musical history of the Church is rich with variety, and the music used in worship should reflect the variety of Christian experience through the centuries. Further, Christian communities should be able to welcome a diversity of people whose musical tastes are not uniform or narrow. The music of the Church, to be true to the Lord of Church, must be able to appeal to all sorts of people. The question of ethnic music in worship has particular relevance here. It is clear that the use of ethnic music can be either ecumenical or divisive: on the one hand, if used with caution and sensitivity, it can enrich a congregation's spiritual life; on the other hand, if used exclusively, as is done, for example, by some of the black-led churches, it does nothing to bridge gaps or enlarge sympathies.

Exclusiveness, for whatever reason, prevents growth to Christian maturity; divisiveness denies the Church's all-oneness in Christ Jesus; both do despite to the present Word.

Bad music is, of course, subject to the judgement of the Word. The definition of *bad* is complex, but it has at least two clear elements; the one is musical, the other is moral. The musical element is perhaps not an appropriate subject for discussion here, except to say that in worship only the best should be offered to God, and the music we offer should be the best that we can produce. But the moral aspect of music is plainly of legitimate concern. Vaughan Williams argued, in the preface to *The English Hymnal* (*1906*) that good taste in music was indeed a moral matter, and it might be added that it is a theological matter. Music that is written to secure a quick and easy return; music that is competitive, that draws attention to itself; music that makes it easy to ignore the words, or worse still, devitalises or contradicts the words is surely unfit for its purpose. If the Church's song be the vehicle of the Eternal Word, and if music help to interpret the Word and to express man's words, then the words used must be expressive of the Word, and the music used to convey the words must be able to carry their meaning. Music which obscures the meaning of the words or which diminishes the reality of the present Word is not music which is suitable for worship. It is, therefore, bad music.

Good music, on the other hand, should not only move us, but should move us to think. It should be able to catch us up in a sense of wonder, to say something new, to make it possible for our duty to be also our delight. And our duty is not to please ourselves, but to worship God. In the worship of God, we should never be seduced by the meretricious because it is trendy, or by the third rate because it is easy on the ear. Thomas Wilson, in lamenting the fact that 'music is nowadays almost universally used not for itself, but as a palliative, a pain-killer' reminds us, in a striking phrase that 'music should be an inspiration, an aspiration, not an aspirin'.[18] An *inspiration*, an *aspiration*, these two precisely describe the role of music in worship. The one implies the presence of God in the worshipping community; the other points to the need for effort on the part of the worshippers, an effort which in turn is inspired and sustained by the presence of the Eternal Word.

It is, however, this very effort which is so often lacking in many congregations and which indeed is resented if an attempt is made to introduce it. Hegel's remark that 'an old woman likes a sermon full of texts she knows, so that she can nod her head wisely when she hears them'[19] is a parable of most congregations' attitude to church music. They like what they know, and are resistant to the unfamiliar. Yet musical idioms, like all other idioms, can be hideously over-worked, and can invest worship with an air of triteness and tediousness, not to say banality, which completely deny the freshness and the vigour of the Gospel. Certainly, Christ the present Word is not well served by the superficiality and complacency of much of our music-making. Of course there must always be a place for the familiar and the much-loved; but unless there is also a place for the dynamically new, the demanding new, we do little to make eloquent his Word who is among us to make all things new.

So far, the discussion has concentrated exclusively on hymn singing, congregational hymn singing. There are still many other areas of church music to be explored, and each of them is subject to the Word present in the worshipping community and the need to allow that Word free course in the assembly of God's people. Anything that restricts or obscures the Word is at the least questionable, and in the last resort is not permissible. A brief glimpse of some of these other areas will suggest questions that need to be explored. The use of choirs is an obvious place to begin. The original, historic function of a choir was to sing the liturgy, and the music was the sacred routine of the daily round, together with the great climax of high mass on Holy Days. The choir was an inconspicuous, faithful servant of the liturgy, allowing the Word full play without distraction or spectacle. So long as modern choirs fulfil something of the same role they are helpful though not essential contributors to worship. But the moment they become obtrusive, or in any way self-seeking, their usefulness to worship is diminished.

If choirs must serve the Word, so too must organists and other musicians. Instrumentalists of any kind are welcome in church, but not to provide a 'suitable atmosphere for worship' (for that can too easily sink into sentimentality), nor to provide a 'musical interlude' (for that can become a vehicle for mere self-advertisement), but to engage in the offering of the worship of the people of God, helping them to perceive the Word in their midst and encouraging them to glorify him and to edify one another.

Choir and instrumentalists together have a vital function to fulfil in the worship of the congregation, by singing the liturgy where that is the tradition, by offering anthems where that is appropriate, by sympathetic leading of the congregation's singing where that is the pattern of the worship. Again, it would be great gain if the original use of the anthem were to be recovered, namely, to signal to the worshippers exactly what is happening Sunday by Sunday; and it would be an even greater gain were the original material to be used, the words of scripture. Indeed, it might not be too much to claim that choir and organist would find a new role if, instead of complex anthems, they took to chanting the psalms week by week. The discipline of psalmody of this kind would not only remove from the musicians any taint of exhibitionism; it would also restore to the congregation a means whereby the Word of God could enrich the worshippers' experience.

The purpose of worship is to restore that sense of communion with God which is the essence of the spiritual life but which is constantly being thwarted, belied, diminished, or encroached upon by everyday life. Worship has many elements, among which the primary one is that it brings us a sense of God's presence, the realisation that he is present, bestowing blessings, giving himself. But worship is also our activity as well as God's: the *sursum corda* points to our participation in and anticipation of the worship of heaven, a worship in which we are personally and wholly involved whenever we meet with the people of God. Further, worship is a social act and not just the sum of our individual offerings. The sentiments and aspirations of the several worshippers flow together into a common stream of mutual support and reinforcement, and together we worship God the Father through Jesus Christ the Son in the power of the Holy Spirit. Music is the ideal instrument to blend all these elements of worship together, the divine, the heavenly, the social. And provided it is music that is faithful to the Word and makes the Word more eloquent, music that is self-effacing and God-honouring, it will enable the worshippers to worship in spirit and in truth. Nothing could be finer than Milton's resolve in *Il Penseroso*, and nothing could be more necessary for a true understanding of worship than the final two lines of this stanza:

'But let my due feet never fail
To walk the studious cloisters pale,
And love the high embowed roof
With antique pillars massy proof,
And storied windows richly dight
Casting a dim religious light;
There let the pealing organ blow
To the full-voiced choir below
In service high, and anthem clear,
As may, with sweetness, thro' my ear,
Dissolve me into ecstasies
And bring all Heaven before my eyes.'

NOTES

1   St Matthew 18.20; 1 Corinthians 5.4; Hebrews 10.25.

2   St Matthew 28.20.

3   St Mark 14.22–25; 1 Corinthians 11.23–26.

4   Colossians 3.16. A.V.

5   1 Corinthians 14.15, 26.

6   *Christian Reflections*, Fount Paperbacks, 1981, p. 124.

7   Ibidem, 'On Church Music'.

8   Ibidem, p. 126.

9   *Church Music and Theology* (Studies in Ministry and Worship) S.C.M. 1959, p. 14ff.

10 Ibidem, p. 14 (Exodus 15.21; 1 Chronicles 16.9; Psalms 68.32, 96.1, 2, 98.1; Isaiah 42.10; Jeremiah 20.13).

11 Acts 2.47.

12 St James 5.13.

13 Ephesians 5.19.

14 Hebrews 2.11–12.

15 *Church Music and the Christian Faith*. Collins 1978. p. 137.

16 *Voices and Instruments in Christian Worship*.

17 *Life Together*. S.C.M. 1954, p. 50.

18 *Liturgical Review*. Church Service Society. Vol V, No 2. (Scottish Academic Press) November 1985, p. 9.

19 Barton, J. E., *Purpose and Admiration*, Christophers, 1932, pp. 252, 253.

6

MUSIC AND MINISTRY

Edward Matthews

The celebration of the liturgy requires the exercise of diverse gifts, or ministries, and this diversity, placed at the service of the worshipping community, is a living sign of the Church, the Body of Christ.[1] Music is a highly specialised and influential gift. Correctly exercised, it has the power of raising worship to sublime heights, but misapplied, it is quite capable of reducing worship to the level of mere superficiality.

It has often been said that music is the handmaid of the liturgy, that it serves, or ministers to the liturgy. While this is undoubtedly true in theory, it is not always so clear in its application, and it is therefore useful to remind ourselves of the true function of music in liturgical worship.

Ministry of Music

First, music enhances liturgical prayer by providing additional dimensions of emotion and intellect and beauty. By the power of music the human person is more completely drawn into the act of worship. For this reason liturgical music best ministers to the act of worship when it is something more than mere *mood* music; though creating the right mood for worship is not to be disparaged.

Second, good liturgical music is that which serves the true meaning of the liturgical action, or the text. For example, the types of music selected for the penitential section of a celebration should reflect the sense of sorrow and repentance which is natural to that part of the liturgy. The same music would not be suitable for an acclamation of joyous thanksgiving. Such a distinction has sometimes been

47

lost sight of in compositions for the Eucharistic liturgy of the Roman Church when the same music is used for totally different parts of the celebration. In particular, the not uncommon practice of setting the *Kyrie, Sanctus* and *Agnus Dei* to the same music, as if those parts of the Eucharist were but different verses in the same hymn, is a real disservice to good celebration.

Third, music ministers to the worshipping community by drawing individuals more closely together. The theme or mood of the music establishes a common bond between people who might otherwise find it difficult to relate to the occasion, or particular celebration. This is more clearly the case when the community participates in the music by singing a text such as a hymn. A well-chosen hymn at the beginning of a celebration can do far more for starting the celebration off on the right foot than a torrent of spoken words uttered by the presider. The discipline of singing the correct words and notes in concert with other members of the community has a powerful uniting effect.

Fourth, music in the liturgy has as its ultimate purpose the more complete participation of the community in the liturgical action. This is a simple conclusion from what we have said above, but it deserves to be stated on its own. By participation we do not necessarily mean that the community should sing all of the rite all of the time. Participation can also take place by listening to a choir or a solo instrument, or by silence. But the music, in whatever form, must serve the community and its worship. To use the liturgy as a convenient frame-work in which to display musical talent is a disservice. The choice of music will therefore be governed by the answer to the question: What will best help the people of this community raise their minds and hearts to God, within the context of this particular liturgical celebration?

Ministry of Musician

The Joint Liturgical Group has already addressed at some length the Church's understanding of ministry and the people who exercise it.[2] The authors dealt in the main with the ordained and other officially instituted ministries, but in a final section examined briefly examples of other ministries which help build up the Church. First to be mentioned in this category was the church musician.

As the liturgical renewal has affected so many Christian churches in recent years, the ministry of the musician has gained greater importance. He or she is increasingly understood to be not so much a remote and distant figure, producing music when necessary, as an important member of the worshipping community, responsible to the others in a key aspect of the liturgy. In other words, it is better if the musician is not only an accomplished musician but a committed worshipper. Would it not be better, in some instances, to settle for a less accomplished musician who is nevertheless a worshipping member of the community than one to whom church musicianship is simply a job? Conversely, there is many an accomplished musician who has not been asked to put his or her talents at the service of the community.

To fulfil the ministry of the church musician, the holder should start from a basis of a faith and worship shared with other members of the community. Following on from that, he or she should discuss and plan the music for the liturgy with some of them. Many have discovered the advantage of establishing a liturgy planning committee which is sensitive to the needs of the community at large. This enables those in specialised ministries, like musicians, to retain a sense of balance and be open to the needs and feelings of the church members. The key word is *service*, and this is best fulfilled if the musician has constantly at the front of his or her mind the priority of encouraging participation in the liturgy by all members of the Church. True ministry starts not from the music but from the overall act of worship.

Such a priority can pose special difficulties for choir leaders and choristers. Participation, as we have indicated earlier, does not demand that the music be reduced to the lowest common denominator. Choral music can enhance considerably the beauty and the cultural level of liturgical celebration, and in this way heighten the spirit of worship of the community. The leader of the church choir should therefore suggest music which is both satisfying to the musical capabilities of the choir and at the same time adds to the community's worship.

Instrumentalists, too, need a combined musical and liturgical sixth sense. Contemporary worship has witnessed the introduction (reintroduction, in some cases) of a wider range of musical instruments. Apart from the organ, the piano, flute, violin, guitar and other instruments have found a place in worship. As long as they are at the service of worship there is no reason why any instrument should be excluded. Most musical instruments most of the time are used for accompaniment, or the support of singing. Instrumentalists can at times be encouraged to perform solo pieces as long as that performance serves the prayer and worship of the community.

A recently revived liturgical ministry is that of cantor. Cantors in the Divine Office and Latin Eucharist have been known for centuries. The modern cantor is more of a leader, will perhaps rehearse the community in its music immediately before the start of a service, conduct the community during it, sing solo pieces such as a Psalm to which the community sings a response, and generally lead worshippers through the musical parts of a celebration. This ministry demands special skills of voice, musicianship and communication. The cantor is frequently able to draw the community into more active participation, while acting as the vital link between the people, the choir and instrumentalists.

In *Getting the Liturgy Right* it was suggested that one cause of amateurish and even incompetent pastoral work was the Church's failure to recognise officially those ministries other than the traditional clerical ones.[3] This stricture must also apply to liturgical musicians. Some, though not all, Christian churches do not take musicians seriously, their ministry being regarded as inessential. To institute an official form of ministry would affirm the worth of the musician, encourage him or her to higher standards of musicianship, and commit the community to the training and support of its music ministers.

Being a liturgical musician is not easy. Frequently we

hear it said that the musician helps others to worship while he or she is so distracted by the responsibilities of the ministry that there is no time to pray. It is not so. The effectiveness of liturgy does not depend upon the pious fervour of the individual, desirable as that may be, but upon our service and support of each other. This, surely, is what Christ's ministry was all about. In theory, he could perhaps have worshipped the Father more fervently without the distraction of redeeming humankind and building up the Church into a sacramental image of himself. In the same way the musician worships best when ministering to the worship needs of the whole community and in so doing builds up the body of Christ on earth.

NOTES

1   cf. 1 Corinthians 12.4ff.
2   *Getting the Liturgy Right*, Edited by J. C. D. Jasper. S.P.C.K. 1982, pp. 6–15.
3   *Ibidem* p. 14.

7

THE MODERN STATE OF THE ENGLISH LANGUAGE

Gordon S. Wakefield

It needs to be recognised at the outset that the science of linguistics is as much a battleground of contending opinions as theology or economics. Robert Burchfield, in his admirable, though not uncriticised, short study, *The English Language*, has said that 'since 1945 linguistics as a subject has been riven and dismembered by disastrous civil wars between eminent scholars, most of them still unresolved, and the theoretical outlook is gloomy'.[1]

The controversies and quarrels which rent the Cambridge English faculty some years ago received publicity in the national press. These were hard for a lay person to grasp except in terms of conflicting personalities. Any thorough examination of the present state of the language would need to enter the enclosed, specialist worlds of linguistic philosophy and structuralism, post-structuralism and deconstruction, in which renowned, traditionalist literary scholars are as little at home as Victorian ladies amid punk-rockers, and 'find no end in wandering mazes lost'. A present fashion would contend that the last person to consider in literary criticism is the author under scrutiny: his background, intentions, meaning are irrelevant. When that is said, the work of philosophers such as Ludwig Wittgenstein and J. L. Austin cannot be ignored in so far as they have helped our understanding of the nature of language and have evacuated its over-furnished, over-decorated house of much bric-a-brac, which may have concealed the bare fabric of truth. Wittgenstein's claim that 'Philosophy is the battle against the bewitchment of our intelligence by means of language' constitutes a warning to all those in danger of being inebriated by words.[2]

At the outset, a personal *parti pris* must be acknowledged. I am a linguistic conservative in that I believe that there was a transcendental excellence in the language of Shakespeare, Milton, the lyrical poets, of Johnson and Macaulay, and of *The Authorised Version, The Book of Common Prayer* and their derivatives, the best of the hymns of Wesley and Watts. This ought not to be lost either in its original sources, or in its continual influence. I am also a *prescriptivist*. I believe that language should be governed by rules which it is a misdemeanour to break. They may be minimal but I do not agree that popular usage in grammar, syntax, or vocabulary must prevail. I cannot be undisturbed by the frequent misuse of the first person nominative, for example 'He was kind to my wife and I', nor can I think it a thing indifferent when *criteria* is used as a singular noun, or when a work published within the last quarter century is called a *classic*. I deplore the passing of *the* classics and in many ways regret that I received a *modern* education. I must confess to fellow-feeling with Evelyn Waugh:

> 'Today I remember no Greek. I have never read Latin for pleasure and should now be hard put to it to compose a simple epitaph. But I do not regret my superficial classical studies. I believe that the conventional defence of them is valid; that only by them can a boy fully understand that a sentence is a logical construction and that words have basic inalienable meanings, departure from which is either conscious metaphor or inexcusable vulgarity.'[3]

There is more here than elitism and pedantry. I cannot but concur with Geoffrey Hill, a modern poet, on the verge of *greatness* according to some, in these sentences from his inaugural lecture in the University of Leeds, in 1977:

> 'It seems to me one of the indubitable signs of Simone Weil's greatness as an ethical writer that she associates the act of writing not with a generalized awareness of sin but with specific crime, and proposes a system whereby "anybody, no matter who, discovering an avoidable error in a printed text or radio broadcast, would be entitled to bring an action before (special) courts" empowered to condemn a convicted offender to prison

or hard labour. It may well strike others as unassailable evidence that the woman was merely an obsessional neurotic. Perhaps one could phrase the matter more moderately and say that one does not regard it as at all eccentric to endorse the view that grammar is a "social and public institution", or to share W. K. Wimsatt's belief in "the fullness of (the poet's) responsibility as public performer in a complex and treacherous medium".'[4]

Thus my own bias. It is time to turn to some of the social influences which have changed the English language since 1945.

(1) The Changes in Society

Egalitarianism, a declining use of titles, an increasing use of Christian names, and greater informality throughout society as a whole, are bound to affect language. The age of jeans speaks differently from one in which the upper classes dressed for dinner every evening as happened until 1939. Susanna Wesley made her children address each other as *Sister Hetty*, and *Brother Jackie*—a great check on hot temper—but this is not the spirit of our age, which is informal and casual and speaks accordingly, and writes likewise, at least in comparison with previous generations.

Some changes go back further than one might think. The replacement of *thou* by *you* occurred around 1600 and by the time of the American War of Independence, *thou* was confined to Quakers, dialects and the language of liturgy and Scripture, while *ye* disappeared from standard speech altogether. Only in the last twenty years have the Churches caught up and made speech to God simpler and more direct through the *you* form. Modern liturgy uses fewer words than its Cranmerian precursors. The liturgical revisions have not won favour among many literary critics and we shall have to notice some of the problems attendant on this and other changes later. There are on the one hand those who still contend that our unique relation to God demands a special even if archaic language, and on the other those who would rejoice that no longer do we approach God as if he were a transcendental Tudor monarch. Few, however, have felt at ease with the original ICET version of *Te Deum*, 'You are God: we praise you', which sounds brazen and which the English Language Liturgical Consultation recommends should be changed to the original English form 'We praise you, O God'.[5]

In liturgy and in hymnody less formal language makes for conciseness though some would argue that this results in worship more businesslike than contemplative. But in society as a whole and in non-liturgical worship our informal age is often very verbose, whether in the late 1960s' vogue for the soliloquies of Michael Quoist, now almost past, or in what might be called *news-headline prayer*, the rehearsal of a long catalogue of items from the day's news as the content of intercession.[6] The barrage of words was never more pulverising, nor the chatter more incessant.

(2) The Media and Spouters' Law

The constant stream of interviews on radio and television, opinions asked from all and sundry, *chat-shows* and panels of politicians and sportsmen, dethrone the monologue and the oration and tend often to ungrammatical and often unfinished sentences. Robert Burchfield has noted a whole range of improprieties: 'false concord (The jury hasn't been able to reach their verdict)'; classical plurals construed as singulars; failure to use the oblique case of pronouns; hanging participles; confusion of *less* and *fewer*; verbless sentences; and emphasis on minor words, the articles or various conjugations of the verb *to be*.[7]

(3) The Abolition of Censorship

Readers have become conditioned to the frank and detailed accounts of sexual relations in which contemporary fiction has indulged over the past twenty years, and which have also formed a prominent part in literary and other memoirs. But the terrible advance of AIDS may result in a new censorship on the part of authors themselves.[8] One would hope that there would not be a return to omission marks: rather, a reaction from crude Rabelaisianism to the classical and early Renaissance awareness of the beauty of human love, the physical expression of the spiritual. 'To the pure all things are pure' and pornography is as often the creation of the reader's as of the writer's mind.

In several words a specific sexual sense has placed earlier general senses at risk, for example *ejaculation, erection* and *intercourse*[9] and, we may add, *gay.* This is a warning for preachers. 'Four-letter' words are no longer excluded from literature of all kinds and are found in modern poets. They do not shock the young and may be defended as honest and realistic—people do talk like this—and if they become part of normal speech and are not inhibited in mixed company, they may no longer be thought indecent. But there may always be an underworld in human society with its own vocabulary, just as there are dustbins and sewers around our habitations, and some of the need for expression may best, like vomit, be kept from the kitchen and the living room.

Language is awesome. Goethe translated *Logos* in the Prologue to St John's Gospel, not as Word but as Deed. Donald MacKinnon has written on *introspection and the language of freedom.*

> 'I could have done otherwise. Such a phrase might express not simply a retrospective glance at what might have been, but an act of repentance which it makes concrete. When the prodigal said that he would arise and go to his father, he was no doubt, from one point of view, recording the fruit of inward communing with himself. But at the same time he was making that communing something more than a mere daydream, and he made it so by linguistic action. He said something to himself, and, by saying, he did something.'[10]

In Scripture sin is often connected with speech and language, the prophet's unclean lips and the constant condemnation of lying, deceit and hypocrisy. There is doubtless worse language than verbal obscenity; and there may be a catharsis in cursing and swearing, which saves from what would be lethal violence. But the word has power and may wound or even kill the spirit or do damage beyond repair in lost innocence, pain and the loss of the ability to think of

God. The words, images and objects of piety may be for-ever tainted by unclean associations.

(4) *Feminism*

The movement for the equality of women has resulted in some general changes in everyday speech. The outlawing of sex discrimination demands that the phraseology of advert-isements for jobs be altered, while to take but one instance of a trend, *Chairperson* is often preferred to *Chairman*. In the Gifford Lectures for 1982, Stephen L. R. Clark some-times uses *she* and *her* instead of the conventionally inclus-ive *he* and *his*.[11] He usually retains the masculine pronoun for God. In the Churches there are many women, mostly professional and intellectual, who have in recent years raised issues of liturgical language of which revisers of the service books and even ardent feminists themselves were innocent a dozen or so years ago. No longer is it tolerable to them to think of *man* in the sense of the Greek *anthropos* as meaning not *male* but *a member of the human race*. Some-times one fears that the one criterion for an act of worship is whether or not it includes *sexist* language and such sensit-ivity may overwhelm prayer and praise and any conscious communion with God. The consequences for belief in the authority of Scripture or even for the finality of the revela-tion in Christ may be serious, Some women are now calling themselves with commendable honesty 'post-Christian feminists'.

There is a rearguard action in which women are promin-ent. Mary Hayter's *The New Eve in Christ* (SPCK 1987) has as its sub-title 'The Use and Abuse of the Bible in the Debate about Women in the Church'. She declares that to add the term Mother to the traditional address of God as Father 'actually encourages the misguided attribution of sexuality to God rather than abolishing it'.[12] Roland M. Frye, Professor of English literature in the University of Pennsylvania, in a long article 'Language for God and Feminist language' written for a committee convened to prepare *A Brief Statement of Reformed Faith* in 1986 avers that to speak of the Motherhood of God leads to Arian and

Gnostic heresy and menaces Trinitarian faith. He points out that the reason why the Bible speaks of God always in the masculine—it uses the feminine only in *simile* and this rarely—is not Patriarchalism but due to the fact that many of the pagan deities were feminine. In this century, the German Christians under Hitler contended for inclusive language in the translation of Scripture because they found it intolerable to conceive of the Jews as a chosen race, or Jesus as a Jew. Ernest Bergmann and others rejected Christianity because 'it seemed to represent the victory of a god with an exclusively masculine character, while humanity has to go back to the Mother-Spirit, opposed to the anthropomorphic Spirit God'. The traditional belief in a Man-God must be replaced by the belief in *Mother Nature*, the *Great Mother*. 'God is dead' as Nietzsche said, 'namely, the manly Creator God. The idea of God must have a bisexual character'.[13] We need, therefore, to beware of talk of God/she and God-ess by Rosemary Ruether and others. It is better to rest in the magisterial phrase of Simone Weil: 'God alone has the power to name himself'.[14]

The matter of 'inclusive language' may not be decided simply in terms of women's rights, nor of the movement for their ordination as priests in the 'Catholic' Churches. In addition to the theological dangers, there is the question of violence to language itself, of mistranslation and of verbal infelicity, all of which, on the presuppositions of this chapter counter offence by offence. There is also the yet more serious question whether our age does not need to recover awareness of the differences between male and female. This does not mean male dominance, though the male's responsibilities are different from the female's as is his body. Partnership in the bringing up of children may be one of the healthiest developments of our time in some social classes. But unless differences are recognised the balance of nature may be as much upset as by ecological interference.

This is not to deplore all attempts in Bible translation and in liturgy to become inclusive; and there are numerous instances where this is easy and obvious without destroying rhythms or perpetrating errors. But there are dangers.

Whether it is right to tamper with texts not of our generation may be disputed. It is better to leave old authors alone, while being as inclusive as possible in what is written today.[15]

(5) The Enlargement of Vocabulary through Technical Terms

A former Jesuit who from 1957 to 1970 was concerned at Farm Street with preparing people for reception into the Roman Catholic Church told me that one of the changes in those years was that at the end of the period it was possible without risk of bewilderment or lack of comprehension to use more polysyllabic and technical words. This is undoubtedly due to the alliance between the applied and social sciences and the media to say nothing of the proliferation of computers, so that a three-year-old boy of my acquaintance could talk of 'an integrated circuit', while some psychological and medical terms are current coin; they would have been Greek at the turn of the century and after. Some writers have become sesquipedalian for the fun of it, like W. H. Auden wearing out the massive volumes of the Oxford English Dictionary and writing of 'an analeptic swig' snatched 'from the bottle in my bag', or Anthony Burgess perpetrating some monstrously recondite constructions. There are words which have their vogue and then mercifully cease to be. *Viable* was everywhere and inescapable in the late 1960s, applied universally from the economy to the spiritual life; *parameters* has been fashionable for some years. But there is a difference between long words, possibly of classical origin, and jargon. Some years ago, *The Times* gave a rendering of the opening verses of St John's Gospel in *OU* (Open University) *Speak*:

> 'At the initial moment in time was a verbalization situation, and the verbalization situation was in the environmental totality, and the verbalization situation was the environmental totality. The same was in an ongoing linguistic doghouse situation.'

This is caricature, but not unjust. It is of a different order from Wesley's occasional classicisms—'Amaranthine, ante-

59

past, panoply' and the like which he persuaded *converted boozers* to sing.[16]

The Sense of the Word 'After Auschwitz'

George Steiner has raised the question whether in the knowledge that a man may read Goethe or Rilke and play Bach and Schubert and then go to his day's work at Auschwitz, we dare claim 'that culture is a humanizing force, that the energies of the spirit are transferable to those of conduct'. Theodor Adorno, a European Jew, has said 'No poetry after Auschwitz'.[17] W. H. Auden declared that while the historian must tell of evil, 'the poet cannot get into this business without defiling himself or his audience. To write a play, that is to construct a secondary world, about Auschwitz, for example, is wicked: author and audience may try to pretend that they are morally horrified, but in fact they are passing an entertaining evening together, in the aesthetic enjoyment of horrors.'[18]

Professor C. B. Cox has said that modern poetry does not produce great epics. And it is not only the evil in the world but scientific discovery that makes us feel isolated in a universe beyond our comprehension. This changes attudes towards language and causes 'a growing uncertainty about words and their relation to things'.[19] This has meant that writers such as T. S. Eliot, James Joyce and Dylan Thomas have tried to extend the limits of language beyond the bounds of rationality. It means on the other hand that a poet such as Philip Larkin has, like John Betjeman, confined himself to ordinary, everyday experience and has refrained from metaphysical flights. Donald Davie has expounded a contractual theory of genre and syntax which must not be broken by the poet creating a private language. Words should keep their everyday meanings in poetry—a notion compatible with Davie's work on the literary tradition of Dissent and his superabundance of the hymns of the evangelical and nonconformist tradition in *The New Oxford Book of Christian Verse* (1981).[20]

But post-war poetry is not always 'an articulation of small non-heroic experiences in small, non-heroic verse'.[21]

In the verse of the Poet laureate, Ted Hughes, we find the savagery of nature and the mythological fantasies of violence. Here are wit and exuberance amid 'nature red in tooth and claw' and 'a deliberate smashing of traditional linguistic forms'.[22] One trembles on the brink of destruction, yet is strangely exultant. There are here two different reactions to the age of Auschwitz. That represented by Larkin takes short views in a universe where the long offer only death; but this may result in a commitment to people who love and suffer and may do more for the immediate future of the world than what Cox calls 'the poses of romantic heroism'.

Since Cox's lecture, Geoffrey Hill has emerged to the centre of the literary stage with his 'superbly burnished' language. He is not plain and perspicuous but is haunted by the fearsome yet sublime images of Christian faith though he would not call himself a believer. He has written what Christopher Ricks has called 'the deepest and truest poems on the holocaust'.[23] He is a poet of reconciliation—*at-one-ment* with a propensity for the hyphen. Maybe there is a certain fascination with horror—he writes more of martyrs than of saints and has something of the 1960s goriness of Ted Hughes, though he is not liberated from the Christian tradition. He is not afraid to use the language of Christian devotion, however little meaning it may have for literary sophisticates today. (And the hostility to his Christian images must not be minimised.) He is antipathetic to Romanticism and spurns a Miltonic 'grand style'. 'There is little explicit sexuality but some language which falls on the ear like music. And words are of terrible weight. They have the specific gravity of sin. It is as though,' Hill writes, 'the very recalcitrance of language stood for the primary objective world in one of its forms of cruelty and indifference.' And somehow 'it is at the heart of this heaviness that poetry must do its atoning work.'

It is said that Hill was once asked to help in a liturgical project, to take certain ideas and turn them into language worthy of worship. He was appalled. Poetry comes by inspiration and then craftsmanship often with agony. It cannot be done to order or for the purposes of propaganda, however exalted.

In conclusion, we may, in spite of those who would prostitute it by ideology, pornography or jargon, claim that the English language still has its vigour and beauty. The continuing devotion of poets to the Word is *stupor mundi*. They are the guardians of the flame which sometimes professing Christians would snuff out. Liturgy must not be undertaken without an awareness of language.

The Alternative Service Book (*1980*) has been much scorned as have new translations of the Bible, with talk of 'Sunday supplement prose' and so on. There are banalities and misguided revisions in the Book. Some of the Collects are not as felicitous as the originals. But David L. Frost has well explained and defended the Eucharistic prayers.[24]

The tragedy of liturgical revision—and the word is used advisedly because there is a sad inevitability about it—is that the disappearance of old phrases of Scripture and the Prayer Book means that we have now no common prayer. Never again will English people be united in thanksgiving or intercession. The preference of Royal brides and bridegrooms for the traditional language of the Marriage Service fulfils one of Baumstark's 'laws' that the solemnities demand the archaic. But there is his preceding melancholy formulation 'the law of organic development—organic and therefore progressive—the more primitive elements tend to disappear'.[25] The loss may have deep effects on the psyche. Many an analyst will testify to the healing power of archetypical language—phrases from *The Authorised Version* or *The Prayer Book* retained in the sub-conscious, which may emerge with salvific effect. Robert Burchfield, so confident about the survival of English as a whole and more a *descriptivist* than a *prescriptivist*, adds to the jeremiads at this point;

'Indeed, when one considers the threading of the traditional language of the AV and the BCP into English literature through the centuries, and the improbability of *any* enrichment of English literature by the NEB and ASB in the future, the loss for society as a whole—not so much of particular words as of the way they are put together—is grievous beyond all knowing.'[26]

The fact is that there is now no common culture. The lament has a dying fall like so many others for past glories departed. Methodists may wonder whether the Wesley hymns will survive in their full richness, since, although they occasionally 'improve' on the AV, they are a tapestry of biblical allusions in the traditional language, and these may become unrecognisable as the new translations are all that are heard or read.

But hymns are not poems in the sense of our discussion. They are often written to order and, as Isaac Watts claimed for his own work, fine phrases and high-sounding sentiments must sometimes be rejected. Yet they must conform to certain canons of prosody and metre. Some of the rhymes of popular muses are execrable. The best hymn writers of recent decades have certainly shown skill, and something of the clarity, simplicity, compassion and *commitment to life* which C. B. Fox found in the Larkin school of poetry. Occasionally there is banality. Fred Kaan's 'Magnificat Now' ends in bathos:

'He calls us to revolt and fight
with him for what is just and right,
to sing and live Magnificat
in crowded street and council flat.'

This is undoubtedly deliberate and Kaan would defend himself; but his is a Magnificat with little praise and of debatable exegesis.

Beyond the simplicities and the social and political preoccupations of modern hymnody there are the great Christian archetypes. And although there may be too much optimism as to the results of Christian action and protest in the world, and sometimes a naive belief in a reconciliation without the Cross so that the wounds of the world are healed too lightly, there is the substratum of the tradition to encourage but also to judge. Christians must not escape into domesticity or shallow optimism in our terrible twentieth century. This is to ignore holocaust for holiday. The only way in which we can come to terms with Auschwitz is through liturgy which sees it and all the unspeakable crimes against humanity in the context of the Crucifixion-Resurrection of Christ.[27] And the language must be modest and shy before ineffable mystery, yet bold to proclaim the victory won.

NOTES

1 Robert Burchfield, *The English Language*, OUP 1985, p. 3.

2 Ludwig Wittgenstein, *Philosophical Investigations*, Routledge and Kegan Paul 1953, sec. 109. See also *Tractatus Logico-Philosophicus*, Routledge and Kegan Paul 1922. J. L. Austin, *How to do things with Words*, OUP 1965; Geoffrey Hill, 'Our Word is our Bond', *The Lords of Limit*: Essays on literature and ideas, Andre Deutsch 1984, pp. 138–159. Isaiah Berlin, *J. L. Austin and the Early Beginnings of Oxford Philosophy* (Personal Impressions), OUP 1982 edn., pp. 101–115.

3 Evelyn Waugh, *A Little Learning*, Sidgwick and Jackson 1973, p. 135.

4 Geoffrey Hill, 'Poetry as "Menace" and "Atonement" ', *The Lords of Limit*, p. 8.

5. See *Praying Together*, ICET 1989, The Canterbury Press Norwich.

6 From the reformation onwards there has been controversy as to whether Intercession is anything but travestied if it is merely a list of happenings, or a succinct series of petitions as in the English Litany (1544) 'short cuts and shreddings which had better be called wishes than prayers'.

7 Robert Burchfield, *op. cit.* pp. 55, 56.

8 See Clancy Sigal, 'Love in Shadow', *The Guardian*, Saturday 7 March 1987.

9 Robert Burchfield, *op. cit.* p. 123.

10 Donald Mackinnon, *A Study in Ethical Theory*, London 1957, p. 129.

11 Stephen L. R. Clark, *From Athens to Jerusalem*: the Love of Wisdom and the Love of God, Clarendon Press, Oxford 1984.

12 *Op. cit.* p. 40.

13 See Adolph Keller, *Religion and the European Mind*, London 1934, pp. 108–9, quoted Roland A. Frye in the paper cited.

14 Simone Weil, *Waiting for God*, London 1973, p. 216.

15 *Pace*, Vivienne Faull and Jane Sinclair, *Count Us In—Inclusive Language in Liturgy*, Grove Liturgical Study 46, 1986. It is noteworthy that Burchfield nowhere mentions this subject.

16 For wise comment on the use and abuse of words and a fine example of the use of short words—which he admits can be boring—see John Sparrow, *Words on the Air*, Collins 1981. For Wesley see Henry Bett, *The Hymns of Methodism in their Literary Relations*, Epworth Press 1913, and subsequent editions, and for early Methodism and 'converted boozers', Charles Smyth, *The Genius of the Church of England*, SPCK 1947, p. 40.

17 George Steiner, *Language and Silence*, Faber and Faber 1967. pp. 15–16, 146. I am indebted for this and the Adorno quotation and much else in this section to a Rylands lecture on 'Recent Poetry' by C. B. Cox, 'Bulletin of the John

to a Rylands lecture on 'recent Poetry' by C. B. Cox, 'Bulletin of the John Rylands Library of Manchester', Vol. 59, Spring 1977, pp. 286–297. See also Christopher Ricks, *The Force of Poetry*, Oxford 1984, p. 287f.

18 W. H. Auden, *Secondary Worlds*, Faber and Faber 1968, p. 84.

19 Cox, C. B., *op. cit.* p. 288.

20 Donald Davie, *Purity of Diction in English Verse*, 1952, *Articulate Energy*, 1955, cited by C. B. Cox. Davie's writing on Dissent is much more recent. *A Gathered Church:* The Literature of the English Dissenting Interest 1700–1930: The Clark Lectures 1976, Routledge and Kegan Paul, 1978, and *Dissentient Voice:* Enlightenment and Christian Dissent, University of Notre Dame Press, 1982.

21 Blake Morrison, 'In Defence of Minimalism', Critical Quarterly, XVIII 2, pp. 43–51, cited by Cox, p. 296.

22 See Ted Hughes, *Crow*, Faber and Faber 1970.

23 See Geoffrey Hill, *Collected Poems*, Penguin 1985. Also Christopher Ricks' two papers on Hill, 'The Tongue's Atrocities' and 'At-one-ment', *op. cit.*, and Alistair Fowler, 'Geoffrey Hill: refined, furious—and great?', TLS 4 April 1986, p. 363f. Also Peter Walker, 'The Poetry of Geoffrey Hill', The Cambridge Review, June 1985.

24 D. L. Frost, 'Liturgical Language from Cranmer to Series 3', R. C. D. Jasper (ed) *The Eucharist Today*, SPCK 1974, pp. 142–167. See Frost's Oxford Movement Anniversary Lecture 1987 at the University of Newcastle, NSW, 'Truth, Language and Liturgy' for a ferocious attack on Feminism and the demand for 'inclusive language'.

25 Anton Baumstark, *Comparative Liturgy*, Mowbray 1957. I have somewhat bowdlerised the law I cite first which is the second of Baumstark's two and states 'Primitive conditions are maintained with greater tenacity in the more sacred seasons of the Church's year'.

26 *Op. cit.* p. 75, 76.

27 *Cf.* Ulrich Simon, *A Theology of Auschwitz*, Gollancz 1967. Nicholas Lash has written: 'I am almost tempted to say that, in the shadow cast by the Holocaust, a shadow eclipsing God in the eclipse of relationship, the Christian *requires permission* from the Jew to sing the Easter "Alleluia" .... The victors, the rich, the powerful, those who call the tune (whether individuals, classes, nations or alliances of nations) always require "permission" to sing the songs of Easter from the vanquished, the poor and the weak.' *Easter in Ordinary*, SCM Press 1988, p. 211.

Since this was written, there have been published Christopher Ricks (ed.): *The State of the English Language*, Faber, 1989, and David and R. C. D. Jasper (ed.) *Language and the Worship of the Church*, Macmillan 1990.

8

SING HYMNS, OR SING LITURGY

Edward Matthews

The celebration of the liturgy 'takes on a nobler aspect' when it is sung and accompanied by music.[1] There will, of course, be notable exceptions to this principle, such as more reflective celebrations by small groups, but it remains true that song, because it engages a wider and deeper range of skills and emotions in the singers, provides an important dimension in worship which otherwise would be lacking. The Vatican's 1967 Instruction says it 'gives a more graceful expression to prayer . . . (and) achieves a closer union of hearts through the union of voices.'[2] Yet song and music should serve the liturgy and respect it; the choice of sung texts and the style of music are to be made within an overall context of the liturgy in general and of particular celebrations. This paper will examine one important aspect of this.

The singing of hymns at liturgical services is a practice which all Christian churches have in common, but the importance of that practice differs from church to church. For the Methodist, for example, hymn singing is an essential element both in the communication and the celebration of the Gospel message, whereas for the Roman Catholic it does not carry the same weight. This difference reflects the underlying liturgical tradition of these churches and is not simply the fruit of a musical tradition.

Broadly speaking, the singing of hymns in the pre-Reformation era was centred upon the Divine Office and services of a devotional and less official nature. The Eucharist contained a hymn only in the form of an occasional Sequence, sung immediately before the proclamation of the Gospel. In the wake of the Reformation, hymn singing increased considerably, especially in the Evangelical tradition. Metrical psalms were in time joined by contemporary compositions, and these were slowly accepted into the worship of some of the more liturgically traditional Christian communities, especially the Church of England. The Roman Catholic Church, mainly because of its use of Latin, retained a Eucharist untouched by the singing of hymns, until the renewal initiated by the Second Vatican Council released a flood of hymns, new and old. Up to that time, Roman Catholic hymn singing was confined largely to semi-official and devotional services.

The question is: should hymns be sung in the liturgy? As the beginning of a response, it must be stressed that participation by the entire worshipping community is a principle upheld by all churches. By making use of a wider range of emotional and artistic expression, musical participation enables the worshipper to become involved in the liturgical action in a fuller and deeper manner than by the mere recitation of words. Music can express subtleties of faith and love which the unsung words only hint at—'He who sings, prays twice'. In addition, the self-discipline required of a community in producing acceptable song contributes to the unity and participation of the liturgy.

The use of hymns depends upon the nature and structure of particular liturgies. The eucharistic liturgies of communities such as the Church of England and the Roman Catholics have built-in texts for singing. Thus 'Lord have mercy', 'Glory to God in the highest', the Responsorial or Gradual Psalm, the Gospel Acclamation, 'Holy, Holy, Holy, Lamb of God', and the like, are texts intended to be sung. In addition, there are texts like the Creed which, though not of their nature demanding to be sung, may appropriately be sung. Other traditions may not use such texts and instead rely upon hymns, chosen for their appropriateness to the occasion.

If the function of a particular liturgical text is that it should be sung, it should not be replaced by a hymn. At first sight the practice of singing a hymn instead of the official liturgical text has a certain attractiveness about it. Congregational participation is high and the text of the hymn is often more intelligible than that of the liturgy.

However this is a short term gain (though for that reason might be acceptable as strictly temporary measure when introducing a congregation for the first time to music in the liturgy). In the long term, the liturgy suffers from a faulty, or incomplete participation, and the worshippers are allowed to drift into a misunderstanding of the nature of the liturgical action.

We are not claiming that hymns are of their very nature inferior to some other forms of congregational singing. Far from it. Even the more traditional forms of the eucharistic liturgy have a place for hymns in contemporary celebration. An entrance hymn, a hymn during the Preparation of the Gifts and at Communion are often most suitable and provide a contrast to other forms of liturgical music in the same celebration. Clearly, the suitability of the chosen hymn will include consideration of the textual theme of the hymn: is this hymn correct for this celebration and this part of the celebration? Its musical form, too, demands consideration: a solemn, dirge-like piece will, quite literally, strike the wrong note on an otherwise joyous occasion.

A corollary of the principle of the correct musical use of liturgical texts deserves consideration and is what we might call 'singing priorities'. This principle requires that when planning particular celebrations, or when planning a community's music long-term, we first plan to sing those liturgical items which of their nature need to be sung. Some traditions see this principle offended when much effort is put into the singing of hymns at the Eucharist or into grand polyphonic choral pieces, while simply reciting items such as the Gospel Acclamation, or 'Holy, Holy, Holy'.

The principles which govern respect for the meaning of the liturgy and the proper functioning of its constituent parts also govern the use of specialist choirs. Christians of the British Isles have every reason to be proud of their choral tradition which is second to none in the world.

Great choral music has graced our churches and cathedrals and enhanced the liturgy for centuries. Yet such music, like all other forms of music, should serve and not dominate. The Vatican Instruction has encouraged the use of choirs in the restored liturgy 'provided the people are not excluded from the parts that concern them. But the usage of entrusting to the choir alone the entire singing of the whole Proper and of the whole Ordinary, to the complete exclusion of the people's participation in the singing, is to be deprecated.'[3] The Instruction goes on to encourage the retention and promotion of the liturgical choir, saying that: 'Its duty is, in effect, to ensure the proper performance of the parts which belong to it, according to the different kinds of music sung, and to encourage the active participation of the faithful in the singing'.[4]

Although the Vatican's Instruction was intended solely for its own Roman Catholics, the principles upon which it is based can be applied to all traditions of Christian worship in which choral music is a feature.

Choirs can bring to the liturgy a beauty and contemplative power which cannot be overestimated, and the abolition of choirs from purely doctrinaire motives may be little more than cultural vandalism. However it should never be forgotten that the choir exists for the liturgy, not the other way around. Liturgy which exists only as a concert setting for the choir and its music may be very beautiful but is liturgy which has lost its way.

Conclusion

The guiding principle is that those planning the celebration of the liturgy should choose the musical form which repects the nature of the liturgy and its individual parts, and which enables the congregation to participate more fully. The liturgy itself is the starting point; this demands that musicians and celebration planners have a good, working knowledge of the nature and function of the liturgy. Only then can they proceed to decide how the worshippers can be enabled to participate fully.

NOTES

1   cf. Vatican II, *Constitution on the Sacred Liturgy*, no. 113.

2   In *Musicam Sacram*.

3   *Ibidem*, no. 16c.

4   *Ibidem*, no. 19.

9

THE CHOOSING OF HYMNS

A. Raymond George

Hymns should be chosen, not by a choirmaster or organist, but by the person who is responsible for the general nature of the service. In many denominations this will be the preacher, even a visiting preacher, for the sermon is the largest variable element in the service and thus sets the tone.

The first essential is that the hymns should be good; but what is a good hymn? Its theology should be sound. Standard hymn books are not likely to contain hymns which are blatantly heretical, but individual choosers may reject a hymn on the ground, for example, that it does not adequately represent the theological position of their tradition.

The hymn should be of good literary quality, avoiding the banal, the trivial, and the sentimental. Henry Bett used to say that there were four main groups of good hymns: the medieval Latin, the reformation German, Watts, and the Wesleys. We might add some smaller groups: a few from the Greek-speaking church, metrical psalms, Caroline divines like George Herbert, dissenters like Doddridge, and so on. The great volume of 19th century hymns contains much that is popular but inferior but also a number of splendid hymns. Our own century, especially the latter part of it, has seen something of an explosion in hymnody, which it is rather too early to judge; but some writers such as F. Pratt Green have written hymns which seem likely to endure.

There has also been in the last century and this a large body of revivalist hymns, songs and choruses. Often, though not invariably, their content is biblical and the theologically sound, but many of them from a literary point of view are trivial, and from a musical point of view so are the tunes which accompany them. Those who dislike them are often accused of being 'high-brow' and snobbish, and it is clear that one must have some respect for what many people find helpful. As a popular expression of praise and devotion they often enrich people's experience of the worship of God; yet, surely, the Church has a duty to offer to God the best of which it is capable, and the word *best* raises the question whether the Church has not a further duty to raise literary and musical standards, and indeed whether, as the word *raise* implies, there are objective standards which go beyond the mere subjective taste about which it is said to be useless to dispute. It is generally held that because God embodies the value of moral goodness there are objective standards in ethics; similarly it may be argued that because he embodies the value of beauty, there are objective standards in aesthetics. William Temple indeed once remarked that the existence of a certain hymn tune was a small but definite part of the problem of evil. It might be replied that ethical judgements can be derived from fundamental precepts such as the command to love one's neighbour, whereas there is no similar criterion in aesthetics, though our Lord's judgement about the lilies of the field seems to favour natural simplicity.

It is also asserted against such objective standards that tastes vary in different cultures. It is commonplace, for instance, that European-style hymns, often in translation, and the corresponding tunes were often imposed on churches in, say, Africa, to the unfortunate exclusion of native lyrics. The population of the Caribbean and the black people of America have always had their own style of spirituals and calypsos which now find expression in the black-led churches of this country. It may be argued that there are objective standards within all these styles, that there are good and bad African lyrics, good and bad spirituals, and good and bad English hymns.

The choice of hymns, always to be made with courtesy and consideration for others, will have regard to the composition of the congregation, including the balance of various age groups. Nevertheless, it would be tragic if the great treasury of traditional hymns were to be lost by neglect. It is sometimes said that their language is largely unintelligible to some people, especially to the young; this is because it is largely scriptural, and some of the terms used in scripture are themselves unfamiliar. But those who aspire to be mature Christians need to learn to understand the Bible, and in doing so they will learn to understand the hymns.

Though choosing hymns for a service is not the same as building a programme for a concert, some of the principles behind programme selection should be followed. The music chosen should provide a representative variety, a diversity of metres, weights and textures, and should reflect both the wealth of the Christian centuries so that one generation can speak to another, and the breadth of the world-wide church. New hymns should be learnt from time to time, and there is something to be said for having hymn practices before the service for this purpose: but there should not be two hymns in one service, both of which seem likely to be unfamiliar.

Some purists insist that a hymn should always be sung to the tune set; once begin altering the tune to one that is more familiar, and you will soon be going round a little tread-mill of over-used tunes. Certainly it is well to learn new tunes, as it is well to learn new hymns. But I see no reason why a tune should not occasionally be changed, for sometimes to sing familiar words to an unexpected tune may call fresh attention to the meaning of the words. Some tunes are put to certain hymns for no other reason than to ensure that they appear in the book somewhere. One must always be sure either that the set tune is suited to the congregation or that some appropriate alternative is available. Some metres are so irregular that no change is possible, and if the tune is not appropriate the hymn cannot be sung. Some excellent tunes are difficult for small congregations.

Who has the last word about the tunes? In most, if not all congregations, this right probably belongs officially to the person conducting the service or to the priest or minister of that congregation. But it is foolish to ride roughshod over the views of organists and choirmasters. It is well for clergy and ministers, even if not very 'musical', to familiarise themselves with names of tunes, understand the use of a metrical index, and acquire such a knowledge of the subject as will enable them to discuss these matters with musicians. As a visiting preacher, often sending notice of hymns by post or telephone, I have found that if I *suggest* any changes of tune which I think appropriate, they are almost invariably accepted.

Much of the art of choosing hymns lies in fitting them into suitable contexts. The question thus arises, at which points in a service a hymn (or psalm or canticle or the like) is appropriate. In what follows, we list the usual places in the Eucharist, or full service of Word and Sacrament. The modern service-books of most denominations roughly coincide in this respect, and we refer at times to the Roman Mass of 1970, (**R**), and to Rite A of *The Alternative Service Book 1980*, (**A**), as a typical modern Anglican rite. The Scottish Liturgy 1982, of the Episcopal Church in Scotland, has no directions about hymns. The material of the hymn book of the Church of Scotland, *The Church Hymnary: Third Edition*, is ordered according to the liturgical structure of the service, and the books of the Free Churches sometimes contain indications about the placing of hymns, but these are not mandatory.

1. **At the beginning.** **R** refers to Entrance Song. If there is no singing, the Entrance Antiphon (Introit) is said. **A** says that at the entry of the ministers a hymn, a canticle, or a psalm may be sung. In fact in all churches an opening hymn, a psalm or the like is almost universal at this point. It may have originated as a 'cover' for the entrance of the ministers, but many would see it as valuable in itself, as uniting the congregation in praise. In the Free Churches it is not usually sung till all are in their places, though it is sometimes preceded during the entry of the minister or preacher by a short anthem or verse of a hymn called the Introit.

2. **Before the readings.** It is a fairly common practice in the Free Churches to have a hymn between the opening prayer and the scripture readings. *The Methodist Service*

Book of 1975 permits a hymn as an alternative to 'Glory to God in the highest', which has the same effect. *Te Deum* might also find a place here.

3. **Between the readings.** R has a Responsorial Psalm after the first reading, and a Gospel Acclamation ('Alleluia' or, in Lent, an alternative acclamation) before the Gospel. If there are only two readings, the 'Alleluia', which includes a verse as well as the actual word 'Alleluia', follows the psalm without a break. The name 'Gradual', originally given to the psalm, is said to derive from the fact that the reader was going up a step (*gradus*) to reach the place from which he read; or possibly because it was read from a step and not from a higher place reserved for the reading of the Gospel. A says after the first reading that a psalm may be used, and after the second, that a canticle, a hymn, or a psalm may be used. A provides two psalms, or portions of psalms, or very occasionally a canticle, for each Sunday and various other days or occasions. It seems to be intended that the first may be used at the beginning and the second between the readings. Many parishes substitute hymns, as is quite permissible, even between the first and second readings, where the rubric refers only to a psalm, for general Direction 12 says that points are indicated for hymns but if reason requires they may occur elsewhere.

Whereas the use of Holy Communion rather than Morning Prayer as the main Sunday service in Anglican churches is much to be commended, this change, and the decline of evening services, has the unfortunate effect that people are less and less familiar with the psalms, but there is at least the possibility of using them at the points indicated. The canticles, however, though very occasionally listed in place of a psalm, have disappeared almost without trace, and there would be much to be said for including them from time to time. *The Methodist Service Book* suggests *Te Deum* especially on Christmas Day, Easter Day, Pentecost, Trinity Sunday, and All Saints Day. It is obviously appropriate on these days, but as they all already have a wealth of suitable hymns, it is not likely to be used. *Benedicite* is suggested especially from the 9th to the 5th Sundays before Christmas, on the summer Sundays after Pentecost, and on Harvest Thanksgiving; *Benedictus* in the mornings and *Magnificat* in the evenings, especially on the Sundays from the 4th before Christmas to the last after *Epiphany; Nunc Dimittis* in the evenings, especially on the Sundays after Christmas; and the Easter Anthems, which in *The Book of Common Prayer*, 1662, are appointed on Easter Day in place of the *Venite*, especially on Easter day and the Sunday after. This advice has unfortunately not been widely followed, but all denominations might well heed it.

This is a convenient point at which to consider the use of Psalms. In the Free Churches they are sometimes used as the Old Testament reading, but more traditionally they form part of the congregation's part in the service in the ways we have already indicated. They are not often sung in the Free Churches, but are sometimes read responsively, though such a reading may be deemed to replace an Old Testament lesson. All the churches, but especially the Church of Scotland, make use of the metrical psalms. Some of these are undoubtedly doggerel, but many of them, widely regarded as hymns, are very popular. An obvious example is 'All people that on earth do dwell' (Psalm 100). Some purists maintain that a psalm, being part of the Old Testament, should not be used at any point later than the point just after the Old Testament reading. The earlier part of the Word service does indeed seem the appropriate place for the psalms, but there are precedents in the Roman Mass for the use of psalm verses at a later point. Moreover, hymn's which in Watts's phrase 'make David speak like a Christian', such as 'Jesus shall reign where'er the sun', based on Psalm 72, are obviously appropriate at any point.

Reference must also be made to Sequences. Sequences are hymns once sung in the Roman Mass on certain days after the 'Alleluia'. Indeed, they are said to have originated from the verses composed to fit a series of notes on which the final 'a' of the *Alleluia* was sung. Even before 1970 only five survived. The number has now been further reduced. There still exist, however, in the current Roman Mass, *Victimae paschali laudes*, which is not metrical, for Easter Day; *Veni, sancte Spiritus*, which is found in modern hymn books in various translations, for Pentecost; and *Lauda, Sion, Salvatorem*, optionally for the Body and Blood of Christ (the old *Corpus Christi*). Curiously, they are put before the *Alleluia*.

The upshot of all this is that most Roman churches will have a hymn at the beginning and a psalm after the first reading, and most other churches will have a hymn at each place; though some, especially Anglicans, may have a psalm in the second place; and some, especially in the Church of Scotland, may have a metrical psalm in one or other of these places.

4. **After the sermon or homily.** R and A have the Creed on appropriate days, after the sermon. Churches which have the Creed at another place or not at all may well feel the need for some response such as a hymn at this point, though the books rarely suggest this.

5. **At the preparation of the gifts.** Here various actions are performed; possibly a procession with the elements and the celebrant placing them on the table or altar, or else the uncovering of the elements. This is often called the *offertory*, but in the Free Churches that term is usually taken to refer to the offering of the money, which indeed in Anglican and Free Churches is often presented at this point. Most books indicate that a hymn or song (*cantus*) may be sung. It often accompanies the taking of the collection and/or the movement of the deacons or elders to their places behind the communion table; but even apart from that, it serves to introduce the Lord's Supper itself or the specifically eucharistic part of the service, and may well have a eucharistic theme. There follows the *taking* of the bread and wine, the first of the four actions in the four-action shape on which Gregory Dix laid emphasis. Though we now see that the first and the third of these are preparatory to the second and the fourth, the fact remains that our Lord performed all of them, and so should we. The hymn will probably 'cover' the *taking* as well as the preparation. Some liturgies, however, do not distinguish the *taking* from the reception

of the elements when they are brought or the placing of them on the table or altar, or they have the *taking* at a different point.

6. **During the communion.** **R** speaks of a communion song or communion antiphon. **A** says that during the distribution hymns and anthems may be sung. *Agnus Dei* has already been said in **R**, but **A** provides that the translation or the paraphrase of it may be used either at an earlier point or during the distribution. In practice a hymn is common at this point, perhaps more so in Anglicanism than in the Free Churches, though early Methodism used hymns to 'cover' long communions. The Free Church custom is, on the whole, to prefer silence or organ music.

7. **After communion.** **A** provides for the optional singing of a hymn before the post-communion prayer or prayers; other books suggest a hymn after the post-communion prayer but before the dismissal, and it seems more natural to have it near to the close of the service. The custom of having a hymn after the dismissal as a sort of recessional is often regarded as an anti-climax, as is the custom of singing a so-called *vesper* at that point.

No one is likely to have a hymn at all these seven points. In practice there will probably be either four or five hymns, though where in the Ordinary of the Mass or its Anglican equivalent, *Kyrie, Gloria in excelsis,* etc. are all sung, the number of hymns is likely to be fewer. It may also be desired to have an anthem or motet and one of the places may be taken for this.

In the Free Church preaching-service, regarded as a sort or *dry* Eucharist, the first four places mentioned above are equally appropriate; but then there will probably follow prayers which include both intercessions and a sort of *dry* anaphora of thanksgiving and dedication, after which will come a hymn just before the dismissal.

In the more old-fashioned type of Free Church preaching-service, where the sermon comes almost at the end, the hymns are likely to be at the beginning, after the opening prayers, between the lessons, and before and after the sermon.

Anglican Morning and Evening Prayer have a different pattern. They provide three opportunities for singing, namely, the psalm or psalms and two canticles. *The Book of Common Prayer*, 1662, suggests an anthem after the third collect, apparently for no better reason than that it is the end of the original structure, to which additional prayers were added. Hymns might seem unnecessary, but when a sermon is added and the Office becomes a major service, it is common to have a hymn at the beginning, a hymn in place of the anthem, a hymn between the additional prayers and the sermon, and a hymn after the sermon. Some object to a hymn at the beginning, as it precedes 'O Lord, open thou our lips', but it seems odd to start a service without a hymn, and indeed *The Alternative Service Book 1980*, says at a point just after the beginning that a hymn may be sung. The Roman Offices, now called *The Liturgy of the Hours*, contain office hymns, now placed very near the beginning, though there is considerable freedom to substitute other hymns. Some Anglican books contain translations of some of these hymns, and seek to use them in the course of the Office, though their Office does not provide a place for them. By custom the place for an office hymn at Evening Prayer is before the first canticle. Some of them can be used at other services at appropriate seasons; among the best known are *Vexilla regis prodeunt* (The royal banners forward go), now in the Roman Evening Prayer (Vespers), in Holy Week, and *Veni, Creator Spiritus* (Come, Holy Ghost, our souls inspire), now at Evening Prayer from the day after Ascension Day to Pentecost inclusive. This last hymn has other uses, as at ordinations. It must also be noted that *The Alternative Service Book 1980*, provides optionally an Eastern Orthodox office hymn before the Psalms at Evening prayer, 'O gladsome light, O grace', a translation of *Phos hilaron*.

Most of these schemes provide four or five hymns for each service. Thus someone who attends regularly one service each Sunday and on a few other days, such as Christmas Day, may sing between 200 and 300 hymns a year;

those, relatively few, who attend twice may sing between 400 and 600. If a hymn is sung less than once a year, it will seem unfamiliar; but if some hymns are sung more than once a year, the total range in use in the course of a year will fall. Are there 600 hymns worth keeping in regular use? Many hymn books indeed contain more, but some of these will be for other occasions, such as baptisms, weddings, funerals, and the like; though baptisms are best incorporated in the main services, and funerals, if not also weddings, cry out for familiar hymns. If then such a book is to be used to the full, something like 600 hymns should be used in the course of a year, though each officiant will probably find some which he does not wish to use. It follows that hymns which are proper to certain seasons should not usually be used on more general occasions. Thus, for example, one should resist the temptation to use 'Come down, O Love divine' as a general hymn; it is likely to be used at Pentecost. When, as often happens, most of the people attend only the morning service, this principle operates the more strongly: if many hymns are used more than once a year, the total repertoire will be not much above 200. R. W. Dale, according to a well-known story, was rebuked by an organist or choirmaster for choosing an Easter hymn on an *ordinary* Sunday, 'But, Dr Dale, it is not Easter'. Dr Dale replied, 'Every Sunday is Easter Day'. It was a good point, but it should not be made in that way too often.

The different places in the service require different styles of hymns. Thus Bernard L. Manning, discussing the choice of 'O worship the King, all glorious above' as a hymn before the sermon, says, 'This is a tolerable rhyme, useful to usher in late-comers, but a most inadequate preparation for the Preaching of the Word'. The first hymn will normally be a hymn of praise; it may well be a metrical psalm. On occasion, it may deal with God's work in creation; then the penitential prayers which follow will represent the Fall, and then will come the Old Testament lesson, followed by a Christocentric hymn, then the New Testament lesson(s); later hymns may then deal with the work of the Holy Spirit, the Church, and the Christian life. Thus the hymns accentuate a sort of chronological scheme which is implicit in the arrangement of the lessons, and also serves to emphasise the three Persons of the Trinity. But such a scheme should not be followed too rigidly.

Where the Roman and Anglican Churches have *Gloria in excelsis*, the Free Churches are likely to have a second hymn, and the general current practice in the morning is that it is a children's hymn. Modern hymn books are to be commended for abandoning the practice of gathering hymns for children and young people in a separate section; children should learn the great hymns of the Church, many of which are relatively simple. Alternatively, as the second hymn follows the penitential section, it might deal with the forgiveness of sins, not to repeat the confession, but to emphasise the joy of being forgiven.

If there is to be a hymn rather than a prose or metrical psalm between the lessons, it might be a hymn about the use of scripture; but there are not enough of these for one to be used every Sunday. Or again, as was suggested above, it might be Christocentric; or it might take up the theme of one of the lessons, and the textual indices in some hymn books are here a useful guide. But a direct paraphrase of a passage just read is probably inappropriate, though it might serve to bring home the point that the hymn *is* a paraphrase, for people may often sing, for example, 'Behold, the mountain of the Lord' without realising how closely it follows Isaiah and Micah.

It is perhaps best for the sermon to follow immediately after the last lesson, but if there is a hymn at this point, it may well take up the theme of that lesson. Indeed that is sometimes an argument for having a hymn here. If, for instance, the Gospel is the Call of the First Disciples, 'Jesus calls us! O'er the tumult' is obviously appropriate. On the other hand, if the sermon expounds that passage, the hymn is equally appropriate, if not more so, after the sermon.

If the Lord's Supper is not observed, the remaining hymns should be hymns of personal dedication, or hymns concerning the Church's mission, though sometimes a hymn of praise related to the theme of the day will be appropriate. But if there is a Eucharist, the question of eucharistic hymns arises. Here differences of theological emphasis affect the matter. Anglicans and Romans will probably distinguish between hymns appropriate at the presentation of the gifts and hymns appropriate during the communion. The former are likely to be general hymns about the Eucharist; the latter, hymns which refer to the presence of Christ, such as 'O Food of men wayfaring'. There are also hymns referring to the offering of the eucharistic sacrifice, many of which may either precede or follow the eucharistic prayer, which on a certain theological view is the offering of that sacrifice. Some of these hymns may not be entirely acceptable in other circles, though the Methodist tradition at least has a very *catholic* notion of eucharistic sacrifice in 'Victim Divine, thy grace we claim', as also in many little-known hymn such as 'O God of our forefathers, hear'. But, just as in the Anglican and Roman traditions there is now more emphasis on the eucharistic prayer as a whole and less on a particular *moment of consecration,* so in the Free Churches the emphasis is on the various actions of the Lord's Supper as a whole, and it is not felt to be incongruous to sing at the presentation of the gifts a hymn which speaks already of the presence of Christ, such as 'Jesus, we thus obey'. There are, however, a few hymns associated with the Eucharist which belong definitely to particular points in the service. 'Ye gates, lift up your heads on high', a metrical version of Psalm 24 and commonly used in the Church of Scotland, goes with the presentation of the gifts and mirrors the Great Entrance in the Orthodox liturgies. 'Let all mortal flesh keep silence' belongs in the Liturgy of St James to the Great Entrance or presentation of the gifts, while 'From glory to glory advancing' belongs to the dismissal in the same liturgy. Some modern hymns also are written for the end of the communion service, such as 'Now let us from this table rise'.

Thus there will often, though by no means always, be a communion hymn at one or other of these places. Generally, however, the last hymn, as at the *dry* service, will be one of dedication, mission, or praise. Some hymns originally meant to deal with the sacrifice of ourselves at the Eucharist are suitable for use as general hymns of dedication, and many hymns written as general hymns of dedication are suitable to the Eucharist.

We come now to the suitability of hymns to the season or theme. On the great days, such as Christmas and Easter, all the hymns will deal with the obvious theme, and it is not necessary to think of progression through Creation, Fall, Redemption, and so on, or to try to relate the hymns to the three Persons of the Trinity. The same may well apply to some other days. It is not enough on Trinity Sunday, for example, just to begin with a well-known trinitarian hymn and to leave it at that. But in the long series of Sundays after Pentecost, as indeed to some extent at the other part of what Roman Catholics now call *ordinary time*, more variety is necessary. Those who follow the Joint Liturgical Group Lectionary, as **A** and several other books substantially do, should be guided by the lessons rather than by the stated theme: for the lessons, though for the most part summed up by the theme, were in fact chosen before the themes were fitted to them. Yet a service in which all the hymns were related to, say, 'The Neighbour' or 'The Proof of Faith', drawing most of its hymns from the same section of the hymn book, would be monotonous. On such Sundays, the hymns should help to provide a wider perspective and set the theme, as does the eucharistic prayer, in the whole context of creation and redemption. For the choice of those hymns which are intended to relate to the lesson, it is helpful to use a textual index such as some hymn books provide.

With this in mind, we may now consider the six seasons into which the JLG Calendar may conveniently be divided. Those who use the Roman Lectionary, and indeed those who follow no lectionary, may easily apply the same principles *mutatis mutandis*.

Pre-Advent and Advent. The ninth Sunday before Christmas deals with creation, and those hymn books which do not have a large section called *General Hymns* usually have a substantial section on Creation, which may well be used in the earlier part of the service. But it would be a mistake to confine the choice to this; later should come hymns on redemption, perhaps on some related aspect such as the new creation.

It would be even less appropriate on the following Sunday to confine the choice to penitential hymns about the Fall. A suitable hymn would be 'Praise to the holiest in the height', but it might be thought that this should be kept for Passiontide. For the next Sunday 'The God of Abraham praise' is an obvious choice.

The hymns for Advent Sunday may well combine the themes of preparation for Christ's first coming and for his final coming. Many Advent hymns are indeed deliberately ambiguous in their reference. Thus, 'O come, O come, Immanuel', links our expectation with that of the old Israel. It is based on the antiphons used in the latter part of Advent, but as a hymn it is appropriate at any point in Advent.

It might be well to begin with hymns of invocation or expectation, such as 'Come, thou long expected Jesus', and move on to hymns of fulfilment such as 'Hark, the glad sound! the Saviour comes'. This principle applies on several other Sundays.

There are several good hymns about the scriptures for the second Sunday in Advent, but in churches where a psalm is not sung between the readings, some of these should be reserved for use before or between the readings on other Sundays.

The last two Sundays in Advent present a problem because of the popular anticipation of Christmas and the expectation that we shall sing *carols*, a word often used to describe Christmas hymns and genuine carols alike. If the third Sunday in Advent involves a toy or gift service, there is some danger of having even Epiphany hymns. To some extent the problem might be mitigated by having *Advent* carol services containing genuine Advent carols and forward-looking hymns, such as 'The race that long in darkness pined' based on Isaiah 9.

Christmas and Epiphany. There is an abundance of hymns and carols. Some are suitable only to the evening of Christmas Eve or to a service at midnight, for example, 'O little town of Bethlehem' and 'Silent night, holy night'. A service ending after midnight might well finish with 'O come, all ye faithful', which would be equally appropriate on Christmas Day; but the last verse, which includes the line, 'Born this happy morning', is best omitted at other times. The service on Christmas Day might well begin with the neglected 'Christians, awake, salute the happy morn', for there is no other occasion when it is appropriate. There are a few other hymns which include the word *today*, but to use them on later days in the same season seems less inappropriate than the use of the Eve or Midnight hymns at other times.

It is a pity if the Epiphany Season is dropped or neglected, but there are not so many hymns for Epiphany as there are for Christmas; they may be supplemented by missionary hymns which take up the theme of Manifestation to the Gentiles. Some churches observe Epiphany on 6 January: others on the first Sunday after Christmas, as in the JLG Calendar, or on the second. These Sundays may also be used for the more theological Christmas hymns, such as 'Let earth and heaven combine', which tend to be neglected at Christmas itself.

The hymns about the Old Year need hardly appear on a Sunday, but a Watchnight Service will include some of them. If it continues beyond midnight, it may well conclude with 'Come, let us anew'. Some hymns about the New Year may appear on the appropriate Sunday. The Presentation in the Temple suggests 'Hail to the Lord who comes'.

After Christmas.   Most churches using the JLG Lectionary have modified it so that the later Sundays after Christmas will be named as Sundays after Epiphany. The baptism of Christ suggests 'O love, how deep, how broad, how high', and there are one or two modern hymns probably written to supply the lack of well-known hymns on this subject. Then come various aspects of the ministry of Jesus, and some more general hymns in praise of Jesus are suitable.

Pre-Lent and Lent.   Themes such as *Christ the Healer* suggest obvious hymns. Ash Wednesday suggests hymns about penitence, but also about forgiveness. 'Forty days and forty nights' is best kept for the first Sunday in Lent, when hymns about temptation are appropriate. The themes throughout Lent reflect a certain restraint and lack of exuberance, but every Sunday is related to resurrection, and gloom should be avoided. Transfiguration, on the fourth Sunday in Lent in the JLG Lectionary, but on other Sundays in the Roman Lectionary and the (American) Common Lectionary, and also observed on 6 August, lacks good hymns; among the best is 'How good, Lord, to be here!'. The theme of Mothering Sunday should not be allowed to drive out Transfiguration. The second Sunday before Easter marks the beginning of what used to be called Passiontide, though Roman usage has now shortened that to a week. A start had better be made on hymns about the cross, for they are numerous, and if they are confined to Holy Week, they will not all be used. The theme *Victory of the Cross* suggests the more triumphant ones, such as 'Lift high the cross, the love of Christ proclaim'.

Palm Sunday calls for 'All glory, laud, and honour', during the procession if there is one, but, if not, at least at some point early in the service. 'Ride on, ride on in majesty' makes the perfect transition to that part of the service which is dominated by the reading of the Passion. Even if the Entry to Jerusalem is read as the Gospel of the main service, there should be some Passiontide hymns. 'My song is love unknown' combines the two themes. The idea of the children of Jerusalem singing the praises of Jesus has produced a number of children's hymns, but there is not much room left for them. The evening service may well contain the Roman evening office hymn for the season, 'The royal banners forward go'.

The JLG book *Holy Week Services*, 1983, suggests for Maundy Thursday a translation of *Ubi Caritas*, namely, 'God is love, and where true love is, God himself is there', which is related to the theme of the foot-washing. Hymns about the institution of the Eucharist are also appropriate.

On Good Friday there is something to be said for starting quietly without hymns in the early part of the service. The traditional service, as set out by JLG in *Holy Week Ser-*

vices, 1983, by the Church of England in *Lent, Holy Week, Easter*, as well as in the Roman Missal and in other books, contains an important place for a hymn to supplement the Reproaches and other traditional material during the veneration or proclamation of the cross. *Pangue lingua gloriosi* is traditional: JLG gives the translation, 'Sing, my tongue, the glorious battle'. There is much to be said, however, for using, 'When I survey the wondrous cross'. The type of service that involves meditations on the Seven Words of the Cross needs hymns, and some books provide hymns for each of the seven words. A Free Church preaching-service needs four or five hymns and there is ample choice. Even on this day gloom should be avoided. It is not simply a day of mourning; it is a celebration of the power of the cross.

Easter, Ascension, Pentecost. The Easter Vigil Service in *Holy Week Services*, 1983, and other such books, is so long that it is not likely to include many hymns. A neglected hymn which makes the same sort of transition which this service makes is 'He dies! the Friend of Sinners dies!'.

Many churches will not have such a vigil, or will have it on the Saturday evening; relatively few will have it early on Easter morning. Very many churches will have a service at about 8.00 a.m. and another an hour or so later. One of these might well begin with 'Jesus Christ is risen today' and the other with 'Christ the Lord is risen today', which in some books is short of its first verse and begins at 'Love's redeeming work is done'. In any case, it should be sung with 'Hallelujah' at the end of each line. There are many other suitable hymns, and a few with references to Emmaus are intended for the evening.

The Free Churches, at least until recently, have not had much idea of maintaining a season. They *drop* Christmas and Easter as soon as the day is over. The more traditional Churches think of Easter as a season, and some hymns about the resurrection, preferably those omitting references to *today*, may be used on the Sundays following; but they need to be supplemented by other hymns of a specially joyful character. The fifth Sunday after Easter has still some of the character of Rogation Sunday, and hymns on sowing and on prayer are appropriate.

There are many good hymns on Ascension, and the service would naturally begin with 'Hail the day that sees him rise'. But falling as it does on a week-day, this festival is very much neglected, and some of its hymns should be used on the following Sunday or they will never be known. If there has been no service on Ascension Day, it is perhaps permissible thus to use 'Hail the day that sees him rise', for to *keep up* a day is less inappropriate than to anticipate it. Many good hymns, such as, 'All hail the power of Jesus' name' are suitable, but some of them must give way to more specifically Ascensiontide hymns, and must themselves be used on other occasions.

It is now fashionable to say that the fifty days from Easter to Pentecost were originally one great festal period embracing the themes of resurrection, ascension, and the coming of the Spirit; the Day of Pentecost brings them to a close, and therefore should not itself be followed by an octave or a season. This has led to the idea that the closing days of the fifty day period should be devoted to the theme of the Holy Spirit. Thus the Roman Catholics now have *Veni, Creator Spiritus* as the evening office hymn at this season, as we have already noted. This may be a good theory but it spells death to the Ascension hymns.

A better course is to begin the hymns about the Holy Spirit at Pentecost and, without making a Pentecost season, to spread the rest of them throughout subsequent Sundays. On the day itself, as on Advent Sunday, it is best to start with invocatory ones, which they mostly are, and conclude with one rather of fulfilment, such as 'Away with our fears'. We have already noted that *Veni, sancte Spiritus* is the Roman sequence for this day; it is thus appropriate before the Gospel.

After Pentecost. There are just about enough hymns for Trinity Sunday, and they may be supplemented by others not always listed under that day, such as 'Bright the vision that delighted'.

Thereafter the more general principles already

expounded are applicable. Special occasions such as Harvest, Remembrance Sunday, All Saints, Saints' days, and so on have their own fairly obvious hymns.

There are of course other services, such as weddings, funerals, confirmations, ordinations, inductions, and the like. Here too the same general principles are to be followed. There are also the sections in hymn books such as *Morning Hymns, Evening Hymns.* These are most useful for occasional use in communities where there is daily worship. Some morning hymns may occasionally be used at the start of Sunday morning worship. Many evening hymns are rather sentimental, but some may be used at the beginning or at the end of evening worship.

A final suggestion is: keep a record of the hymns you use, and look back at the end of a year to see what good hymns you have omitted and what favourite hymns you have used too often.

BIBLIOGRAPHY

Hymns and Psalms: A Methodist and Ecumenical Hymn Book. Methodist Publishing House, London, 1983.

Companion to Hymns and Psalms, edited by Richard Watson and Kenneth Trickett, Methodist Publishing House, 1988.

Partners in Praise, edited by Fred Pratt Green and Bernard Braley. Stainer and Bell Ltd and Chester House Publications on behalf of The Methodist Church Division of Education and Youth, 1979.

The Hymns of Wesley and Watts, Bernard L. Manning, Epworth Press, London, 1942. Reprinted as paperback in 1988.

10

THE ARRANGING OF HYMN BOOKS

Colin P. Thompson and *Gordon S. Wakefield*

Hymns are alive and well in the second half of the twentieth century, despite the apparent decline of institutional church life in Great Britain. Several main hymn books were produced in the 1950s and 60s, a spate of supplements has followed them from the late 60s till the present time, and a new generation of main hymn books has been published in the 1980s. This surge in creativity has produced one of the great hymn-writing periods of the Church. The ecumenical movement has enabled denominational hymnody to be enriched from an ever wider variety of sources, including the growing Churches in the developing world. New kinds of music associated with centres of pilgrimage (notably Taizé and Iona) are also making their mark. *Songs of Praise* and similar programmes reach audiences of millions, and have recently shown a more adventurous and international approach. People sometimes lament that Churches have been reluctant to work together to produce a truly ecumenical book, but it is also important to recognise the gifts present in diversity and to realise that books of all traditions have become increasingly ecumenical in terms of their content—ecumenical across time, space and tradition.

All editors of hymn books have to decide in what sequence to arrange the material they choose. Their decisions can prove illuminating, since the structure of a book can show a Church's sense of the place of hymns in its life and reflect broader liturgical and theological changes which have been taking place.

The simplest solution is to place hymns in alphabetical order of first lines. This, however, reveals nothing about the overall concept of the book, or how the hymns are to be used. The most popular contemporary example is *Mission*

Praise (1983), originally 'compiled to enable the uniting power of music to operate during and after Mission England'. It gives no indication of when the hymns it contains might most appropriately be used during worship or in the course of the Church's year, and it is hard to avoid the conclusion that the book sees its hymns, songs and choruses in the book as fillers. Choice will be governed more by what is popular and well known to a congregation than by the kind of text or music which will enable the people to share more deeply in a particular moment in the service or move from one act to another. It should be noted, however, that *Mission Praise No. 2*, published in 1987, contains a wide variety of material, including hymns for the major Festivals. The alphabetical principle is often followed in supplements to main hymn books because of their relative brevity: *100 Hymns for Today* (1969), *More Hymns for Today* (1980; both Anglican) and *New Church Praise* (1975; United Reformed Church) all use it, but, unlike *Mission Praise*, they have extensive indices which enable the leader of worship to make an intelligent selection.

There are several more considered ways in which hymns can be ordered: according to the biblical pattern of revelation; following a theological understanding of God, the Church and the world; in a liturgical sequence, from the opening to the closing acts of worship; or in a calendrical or seasonal cycle, according to the major feasts of the Church's year. No scheme can be perfect; all are to a degree artificial. Hymns are not written to fit schemes; schemes are worked out to provide coherence and direction for an otherwise random collection. Many hymns could happily be placed in a number of sections in a book, and editorial decisions about their placing can affect how they are used. Isaac Watts's 'When I survey the wondrous Cross' is widely used and loved as a Passiontide hymn, but how many people have sung it as he intended, as a hymn for the Lord's Supper? Christina Rossetti's 'Love came down at Christmas' is usually thought of as a Christmas hymn, but it can be used very effectively for weddings. Many books recognise this by providing cross-references of alternative hymns for each section.

Nor are schemes likely to be followed exclusively. Many books combine elements of two or three, beginning perhaps theologically or seasonally and moving to a liturgical pattern or, less happily, general hymns. There are choices to be made within sections, too: books with a well-developed overall scheme may order hymns alphabetically or chronologically by authorship in the majority of the sections; in others, a biblical or liturgical sequence will be adopted. It clearly makes sense for hymns in the Passiontide section to follow the sequence of events of Holy Week, and for those in the Eucharistic section to distinguish between hymns for before and after Communion. Nor should it be thought that a liturgical or biblical arrangement is not a theological one, and vice versa. Some hymns almost demand sections of their own, while every editorial committe knows how the Christmas section, in use for a relatively short period of the year, quickly becomes so over-subscribed that not everything which might merit inclusion can be found a place. There is a great wealth of hymns for the Eucharist, but a corresponding dearth of really fine baptismal hymns.

An outstanding example of a biblically-ordered book is *Rejoice in the Lord* (Reformed Church in America, 1985), included here because it was the last hymn book the great English hymnologist Erik Routley edited:

PART I: THE GOD OF ABRAHAM PRAISE

A. IN THE BEGINNING
   1. Creator of Heaven and Earth;
   2. The Earth Is the Lord's
   3. Who Pardons All Your Iniquities
   4. God of Abraham, Isaac, and Jacob
   5. Full of Grace and Truth

B. PRAISE THE LORD
   1. Psalms Praise Him
   2. Come, Magnify the Lord with Me
   3. Trust in the Lord

C. THE GLORY OF THE LORD SHALL BE REVEALED
   1. Thus Says the Lord
   2. Comfort! Comfort! My People

PART II: BEHOLD THE LAMB OF GOD

A. HE BECAME FLESH
   1. Advent
   2. Nativity
   3. Epiphany and Youth
   4. Ministry:
      (a) Baptism and Temptation;
      (b) Signs and Wonders;
      (c) Teaching

B. CHRIST HAS DIED! CHRIST IS RISEN
   1. Passion and Death:
      (a) Triumphal Entry;
      (b) Last Supper;
      (c) Crucifixion
   2. Resurrection and Ascension:
      (a) Resurrection;
      (b) Ascension

C. THE SONG OF THE LAMB
   1. Worthy is the Lamb
   2. Jesus Christ is Lord

PART III: SPIRIT OF TRUTH, SPIRIT OF POWER

A. THE HOLY SPIRIT WILL COME UPON YOU
   1. Pentecost
   2. Gifts and Power
   3. Scriptures

B. THE FELLOWSHIP OF THE HOLY SPIRIT
   1. The Church's Founding
   2. The Church's History
   3. The Church's Unity and Fellowship
   4. The Church's Ministry and Mission

C. CHILDREN OF THE SPIRIT
   1. The Christian as Believer
   2. The Christian as Disciple
   3. The Christian as Witness
   4. The Christian as Neighbour
   5. The Christian as Citizen

PART IV: THE HOPE OF GLORY

A. THERE REMAINS A SABBATH: The Church at Worship and Prayer
    1. General Worship
    2. Church Music
    3. Special Times of Worship
    4. Marriage, Family, Friends

B. TOKENS OF ETERNITY: The Sacraments
    1. Baptism
    2. The Lord's Supper;

C. EVERLASTING FELLOWSHIP
    1. Cloud of Witness
    2. Heavenly Company

D. LORD OF LORDS
    1. Enthroned Eternally
    2. Coming in Glory

E. FULLNESS OF GOD

Not for nothing is *Rejoice in the Lord* subtitled 'A 'Hymn Companion to the Scriptures'. The revelation of God in the Hebrew Scriptures is treated seriously, and the Old Testament hope in Part I section C leads naturally into the Advent hymns at the beginning of Part II, which tells the whole story of the Word made Flesh. The third part begins with Pentecost and moves outward to embrace the life of the Church and the calling of every Christian to discipleship—the continuation of the Acts and the Epistles. The problem many books have of where to place the large number of hymns about Christian living is solved by relating them firmly to life in the Spirit. The final part begins with hymns for various services and for the sacraments, and by placing them here suggests an understanding of worship as the meeting-place of earth and heaven (Genesis 28.17) which we more usually associate with the Orthodox. It culminates in hymns of the new Jerusalem and the life of God into which his faithful people will enter, so completing the journey from Genesis to Revelation.

The Church Hymnary: Third Edition (Church of Scotland, Presbyterian, Church of England, Presbyterian

Church in Ireland, Presbyterian Church of Wales, 1973) follows a generally liturgical pattern:

I. APPROACH TO GOD
The House of God
The Majesty of God
Morning
Evening
Confession and Supplication
Invocation
Illumination
Holy Scripture

II. THE WORD OF GOD: HIS MIGHTY ACTS
Creation and Providence
The Promise of the Messiah
Christ's Incarnation
Christ's Life and Ministry
Christ's Passion and Cross
Christ's Resurrection and Exaltation
Christ's Reign and Priesthood
Christ's Coming with Power
Pentecost
The Holy Spirit in the Church

III. RESPONSE TO THE WORD OF GOD
Adoration and Thanksgiving
Affirmation
Dedication and Discipleship
Stewardship and Service
Witness and Encouragement
Intercession:
    For the Church
    For the Church's Mission
    For the Nation
    For the Family
    For the Ministry of Healing
    For Travellers and the Absent
The Church Triumphant

IV. SACRAMENTS
Holy Baptism
Holy Communion

V. OTHER ORDINANCES
Confirmation
Ordination
Marriage
Funeral Services
Dedication of Church Buildings

VI. TIMES AND SEASONS
New Year
Spring
Summer
Winter

VII. CLOSE OF SERVICE
Close of Service
Evening
Doxologies

VIII. PERSONAL FAITH AND DEVOTION

Whereas previous Presbyterian books, (for example, *The Church Hymnary* of 1898 and *The Revised Church Hymnary* of 1927) had not included psalms—a separate and complete metrical psalter accompanied the hymn books—in the *Third Edition* they are distributed among the sections. This caused comment and some consternation, since the metrical psalter has been an essential feature of Presbyterian worship. The inclusion of hymns of dedication, service and intercession following Part II (the Word of God) marks a shift which has been taking place in Reformed and Methodist worship away from the sermon as the climactic act of worship towards placing it closer to the readings from Scripture in the middle of the service, to be followed by acts of response. Sections V and VI do not really fit the liturgical pattern, while the inclusion of a relatively large body of hymns for personal use (33 in a book of 695) invites the suspicion that editors may use such sections as a device for relegating some hymns they would like to have omitted but have not dared to because of their popularity.

There is no official hymn book for the Church of England and to some extent to this day its books reflect the different Anglican parties and theological emphases. The Prayer Book spirituality of a 'godly righteous and sober life' does

95

not tend to lyricism in religion—apart from the fact that Cranmer was no poet. It was a combination of the Evangelical revival and the Romantic movement which forced modern hymnody upon Anglicanism, together with its popular appeal. *Hymns Ancient and Modern*, first published in 1861, remains the standard Anglican book. Its revised edition of 1950 is marvellously comprehensive but something of a rag-bag in its ordering. Liturgy rather than theology controls it, with its first section devoted to times and seasons and the Christian year, with the Divine Office as well as the fasts and festivals a governing influence. The large section of *General Hymns* has a theological arrangement beginning with the Holy Trinity and then the Persons in turn, followed by the Family of God (the Church), two hymns on the Ministry of Angels, and a section on the Christian life, which if compared with that in all the 'Wesleyan' books even up to 1983 would furnish a fascinating study of the contrast between Anglican and Methodist spirituality. A section of 22 hymns of personal devotion consists mostly of Victoriana, though it has Baxter's 'Lord, it belongs not to my care' and some verses from Wesley's 'Wrestling Jacob'. The choices seem a trifle arbitrary except that they are almost all in the first person. The rest of the book is arranged according to the requirements of worship, for the Sacraments, Institutions, special occasions, emergencies and then Saints' and Holy Days, litanies and processions, interrupted by national hymns. The new *Standard Version* (1985) is of similar arrangement, concluding with the supplements *100 Hymns for Today* and *More Hymns for Today*, disappointingly left in alphabetical order instead of being incorporated into the main schemes.

The *English Hymnal* of 1906, compiled by a very able team of hymnologists and musicians, is catholic and designed for Anglo-Catholic churches with Mass, medievalism, plainsong, together with what Erik Routley called a 'boisterous dogmatism' in its more modern words and music. Its contents are not dissimilar from those of *Hymns Ancient and Modern*, though they presuppose a more elaborate ceremonial at a time when Anglo-Catholicism, the age of persecution over, was entering its triumphalist phase.

Hymns were not essential to the progress of worship; they were embellishments of the liturgy to edify the people and 'cover' other activities. The *New English Hymnal* (1986), like the original, has its section of general hymns in alphabetical order. There is no attempt, as in *Hymns Ancient and Modern* to classify them in terms of the stages and experiences of the Christian life.

There are Evangelical collections, notably the *Anglican Hymn Book* (1973), replacing two earlier ones, and *Hymns for Today's Church* (1982; 'the greatest hymns of every age in the language of today'). The latter raises much controversy and is guilty of some banal emendations, but in content both are controlled by evangelical experience rather than liturgy, though there is not the Wesley hymnody of the pursuit of perfection, with its Eastern Orthodox rather than Western Catholic affinities.

We must notice two hymn books, predominantly Anglican in compilation and ethos, which were devised with worship outside as well as inside church in mind. *Songs of Praise* (1925) was the work of some of the editors of the *English Hymnal*. It is in nine sections: *Times and Seasons; the Christian Year; the Communion of Saints; Social Service; General; Special Occasions; for Children; Processional; Doxologies.* The general hymns—that category which to a large extent surrenders any attempt to relate hymns to spirituality—are, as with the *English Hymnal*, in alphabetical order. Professor Donald MacKinnon has said that the use and influence of *Songs of Praise* should be a subject for academic research; but that is not our concern. Some of its amendments and inclusions are unhappy.

The *BBC Hymn Book* (1951) was produced for the Daily Service on sound radio, to accompany the books of prayers *New Every Morning* and *Each Returning Day*. It is used in some parish churches and cathedrals. It is conventionally arranged for worship, though owing to the exigencies of broadcasting none of the hymns is too long, which has resulted in some shortenings, to the deprivation of theology and spirituality.

Hymn singing at Mass is a relatively new phenomenon for Roman Catholics. The coming of the vernacular liturgy has made room and created a demand for hymns and songs which were previously not needed. Modern Catholic books borrow freely from Anglican and Protestant hymnody, as well as from authors of the patristic and medieval periods, sometimes newly translated. The *New Catholic Hymnal* (1971), while a good deal shorter than the standard books of other Churches, is perhaps more suited to 'quires and places where they sing' than to congregations becoming accustomed to singing hymns, as it contains a number of difficult, though beautiful texts, and tunes specially composed. It irritated some people because the editors altered traditional words, mostly in order to avoid unnecessary archaisms. The hymns are placed in alphabetical order rather than being grouped according to liturgical season or special occasions. The editors hoped thereby to avoid restricting their usefulness and to allow new hymns to be examined on their merits, fearing that otherwise people would choose only old favourites from each section. On the whole, modern Catholic hymnody has been left more to its publishers than controlled by committees of church musicians and liturgists. *Celebration Hymnal* (1976), *Song of the Spirit* (1978) and *Hymns Old and New* (1983) have become widely used in Catholic worship, and contain traditional hymns as well as songs influenced by folk music.

Methodist and Reformed Churches, theoretically at least with freer forms of worship than Anglican and Catholic Churches, characteristically take a very ordered approach to compiling hymn books, since hymns are the principal means of congregational participation and may themselves express the liturgical structure of the service. An opening hymn of praise or adoration, followed by hymns of penitance, illumination, affirmation and offering, and with hymns for sacraments and other ordinances included at appropriate points, will enable congregations to share in the drama of worship. The most serious attention to hymn book schemes has naturally enough come from those Churches to whom hymns mean the most. In order to see how changing approaches to hymnody reveal wider changes in theology and practice it is useful to turn to examples from these traditions.

The Wesleys, beginning before their 'evangelical conversions' in 1738, published at least six hymn books for all circumstances of worship and of life, but the collection which governed all subsequent volumes, with very few exceptions, among all branches of Methodism for over a century, was that of 1780, *A Collection of Hymns for the Use of People called Methodists*, which John Wesley described in his preface as 'a little body of experimental and practical divinity'. This the table of contents illustrates:

PART I
    I Exhorting Sinners to Return to God
   II Describing 1. The Pleasantness of Religion
                     2. The Goodness of God
                     3. Death
                     4. Judgement
                     5. Heaven
                     6. Hell
  III Prayer for a Blessing

PART II
    I Describing Formal Religion
   II Describing Inward Religion

PART III
    I Praying for Repentance
   II For Mourners Convinced of Sin
  III For Persons Convinced of Backsliding
  IV For Backsliders Recovered

PART IV
    I For Believers Rejoicing
   II For Believers Fighting
  III For Believers Praying
  IV For Believers Watching
   V For Believers Working
  VI For Believers Suffering
 VII For Believers Seeking for Full Redemption
VIII For Believers Saved
  IX For Believers Interceding for the World

PART V
    I For the Society Meeting
   II For the Society Giving Thanks

III For the Society Praying
IV For the Society Parting

There is no other hymn book like this, and there may be in it the genesis of that Wesleyan custom of using the hymn book not only for public praise but for private devotion. It had its vicissitudes at the hands of early revisers and editors; and it is for societies rather than a Church, so that, as Methodists came to worship independently, there was an ever-increasing need to add to it to include hymns for the Christian year and the various ordinances of religion. Charles Wesley was also a principal source here with his hymns on the objective truths of the Gospel and the Sacraments, but other authors were richly available. The Weslayans essayed a supplement in 1831 and a more extensive one in 1875. This latter begins with *Select Psalms*, all paraphrases, often by Watts and Wesley, a few *metrical*, followed by *Hymns of Adoration* and sections on the Lord Jesus Christ, the Holy Spirit, Penitence and *The Experience and Privilege of Believers*, which continues, with Wesley and other writers, Part IV of the 1780 collection. Then come *Christian Ordinances and Institutions; Death and the Future Life* and *Various Seasons and Occasions*.

In 1904, the Wesleyan Church undertook a complete recasting, which in effect incorporated the 1875 supplement into Wesley's collection, with much editing and many omissions. The order of the contents was entirely in terms of congregational worship. There is first *The Glory of God*, which covers adoration, the Trinity, the divine attributes, creation and providence, Christ from birth to the establishment of his reign on earth, the Holy Spirit and the Holy Scriptures. Then follow *The Gospel Call* and *The Christian Life*, in which the book corresponds most closely to 1780. The remaining sections are *The Church, Time, Death, Eternity, Family Religion*, and *Special Occasions*. At the end come *Ancient Hymns and Canticles*, which contains The Prayer Book canticles, the Commandments and the Beatitudes, obviously intended for those churches where the Order for Morning Prayer was in use, though including the Evening canticles too.

The first of the hymn books of the non-Wesleyan bodies was produced in 1800: *A Collection of Hymns for the Use of the Methodist New Connexion; from various authors; designed as an appendix to the Large Hymn Book* (i.e. Wesley's of 1780). This had the particular purpose of providing hymns for the different parts of public worship, with the very interesting comment that this would make up 'a deficiency in the Large Hymn Book which has often been lamented'.

The books of the other Methodist bodies of the nineteenth century, which became the United Methodist Church of 1907, notably the Bible Christians of 1815, were all dependent on the 1780 collection, though as the century progressed they included new hymns, some of which are inferior poetry, but which were found easy to sing and useful in teaching doctrine. Methodism not least in those branches which were least 'high church' and clerical, sang the faith of the historic creeds and, in hymnody, could not exist on personal experience alone.

Primitive Methodism, a revivalist movement, was perhaps less loyal to Wesley, the bearers of whose name seemed autocrats who would quench the Spirit. It was more concerned that its hymnody should celebrate and contain the experiences of its own revival. It owed much to the compositions of its founder, Hugh Bourne, and to the 'spiritual songs' of the American revivalists, whose methods it copied. Its early hymn books were, in its own idiom 'mission praise'—for example, Hugh Bourne's *General Collection of Hymns and Spiritual Songs for Camp Meetings* (1809 and 1819), and *The Small Hymn Book* (1821). Bourne's *Larger Hymn Book for the Use of the Primitive Methodists* (1824) was part of the process of the evolution from revival to Connexion to Church, signified not only by a nationwide organisation but by missions overseas. In 1886 there was published a hymn book, theologically ordered for established congregations, to which in 1912 was added a supplement, which has been described as 'a collection which catches the somewhat exuberant and romantic atmosphere of Edwardian Methodism'.

In 1933 a hymn book was published for those Methodist

bodies now merged in the Methodist Church of Great Britain. It was destined to last for fifty years. Its table of contents follows closely that of the Wesleyan book of 1904 with one or two transpositions and changes of title of no doctrinal significance except for the abolition of the section headed *Time, Death, Eternity* and its inclusion at the end of the section *The Christian Life* under the caption *Death, Judgement and the Future Life*. There are still echoes of 1780. At the end are *Ancient Hymns and Canticles*, some of the latter provided for churches without the *Book of Offices*. And for the first time there are psalms, somewhat arbitrarily chosen by a 'committee' consisting of a sole Primitive Methodist minister.

The latest book (1983) started out with hopes that it might become the British *ecumenical* hymn book, which word occurs in its title. This hope, unfulfilled, has influenced its contents and made it less 'Wesleyan', though the Wesley hymns include some omitted from 1904 and 1933 and have been edited with greater knowledge and skill than in the latter. It is inevitably as much a period piece of the late twentieth century as the various supplements were of the Victorian or Edwardian periods. The plan of the contents is neat and new, influenced by the hymnological scholarship of the years since the Second World War and much less Augustinian in theology and individualistic in piety. It is theocentric in its three main divisions *God's Nature; God's World; God's People*. The subsections under the first are *A*. The Eternal Father, *B*. The Eternal Word, *C*. The Eternal Spirit; under the second, *A*. The Natural World, *B*. The Social Order; under the third, *A*. A Pilgrim People, *B*. The Worshipping People, *C*. The Christian Life, *D*. The Calling of the Church. There is a large increase in the number of Eucharistic hymns, though the title 'The Lord's Supper' is retained. In spite of the modern interest in spirituality, the section on the Christian life comes much later in the book than in 1904 or 1933 and is reduced to 102 hymns as against 266 in the latter, though the different arrangement may make the figure difficult to establish; but there is no doubt about the emphasis being on social and corporate witness rather than on individual experience compared with previous books in the Wesley tradition. Imperialist hymns are gone, and so, alas! are some classics about heaven. There are many new hymns, notably by F. Pratt Green.

Hymnody among Congregationalists shows other kinds of change. In its beginnings, it was influenced primarily by the French and German Calvinists' metrical psalters, and some of their tunes survive to this day, often closer to their original forms and rhythms than in the nineteenth century, when they were 'straightened out'. The Lutheran Reformation made less of an impact, though in due course many words and chorale melodies found their way across the North Sea, and the towering genius of Johann Sebastian Bach came to be recognised. The work of the Wesleys in the eighteenth century and of translators such as Catherine Winkworth in the nineteenth were especially important in familiarising British congregations with these traditions. The founding father of Congregational hymnody, Isaac Watts (1674–1748), reflects in his own life and work the shift away from singing only the words of Scripture (i.e. metrical psalms and paraphrases) to more personal creations, though still richly imbued with Scripture and often forming dense patterns of allusion to texts across the whole range of the sacred books which create their own kind of exegesis. Watts argued from both Scripture and Tradition that it was proper for Christians to sing the Psalms as David would have sung them had he seen Christ; hence there was room for new hymns to be incorporated into Christian praise. There are still small groups of Reformed Christians who object to this *man-made* hymnody and will sing only psalms (and paraphrases.) The 1952 psalm book of the Reformed Presbyterian Church of Ireland, for example, prints metrical versions of each of the 150 psalms in their biblical order, but divides the tunes into the kinds of mood for which they are most suitable. Such churches also tend to object to the use of musical instruments, believing that the unadorned human voice alone can praise God adequately. The psalm-singing of the Gaelic-speaking congregations of the Church of Scotland and the Free Church of Scotland is unlike anything else to be heard in our islands and reminds us of the persistence of ancient traditions. In this respect, they are at one with the Orthodox Churches, which have likewise never accepted the use of musical instruments.

The last century will have seen the publication of four main hymn books for Congregationalists and their successors in the United Reformed Church. The large corpus of hymns by Watts had, like Wesley's for Methodists, remained staple fare for Congregationalists, with occasional supplements, the last of which was *The Congregational Hymn Book* (1836), hard on the heels of the formation of the Congregational Union of England and Wales (1832). Henry Allon, author of the canticle *Salvator Mundi*, edited the *New Congregational Hymn Book* of 1859, together with *The Congregational Psalmist*, later supplemented with chants and anthems, as musical standards improved and the influence of Anglican worship made itself felt. He also produced words and tunes for children's use. The work of William Garrett Horder 'who did most to create a more catholic attitude towards hymns'[1] familiarised Congregationalists with a much wider selection of hymns, and influenced G. S. Barrett's *Congregational Church Hymnal* of 1887. This begins on a grand scale, with worship and praise of God, and God's creation, providence and redemption. The second part covers the work and person of Jesus Christ, beginning with his divine nature and his Incarnation, and moving through the Gospel story to his Second Advent and Judgement. A final section is entitled *His Names, Mediatorial Titles, and Offices*, reflecting an ancient tradition, both catholic and reformed, of devotional meditation on the many names of Christ in both Old and New Testaments. It is one of the last survivors of the long history of allegorical exegesis, especially of the Old Testament, for many names have their origin in prophecy or in the exquisite poetry of the Song of Songs. Later books refer more simply to his 'Character and Glory', though some hymns on the Names have retained their popularity. There follow hymns of the Holy Spirit, and a short section of hymns to the Trinity. The theological scheme now gives way to a more experimental and evangelical one. *The Holy Scrip-*

tures and *The Gospel and its Invitations* lead into the largest single section. *The Christian Life*, with no fewer than 23 sub-sections, including two hymns specifically devoted to the ministry of angels. The ordering suggests the 'gathered' ecclesiology of Congregationalism, for the Scriptures and the Christian life precede to the next section, *The Church of Christ*. This includes hymns specific to the Congregational way—for Church Meetings, and election of deacons. The remaining sections are entitled *Public Worship, Christian Missions, Special Occasions, Special Intercession, National Hymns, Special Seasons* (times of day, and natural, not liturgical, seasons), *Benedictions and Doxologies* and *Children's services*. There is no real theological plan here. Missionary and national hymns contain several items which would be found absurdly paternalistic or nationalistic now: this was, after all, the heyday of Empire. *Mission to the Jews* and *Colonial Missions* each have a special hymn, while Watts's 'Shine, mighty God, on Britain shine' survives, alongside hymns of intercession for times of drought, flood and pestilence. The book also includes a large selection of metrical litanies, canticles, psalms and passages of Scripture pointed for Anglican chanting, and 120 anthems. It is clear that Congregational worship has undergone an enormous transformation compared with 50 years previously. In spite of the curiosities in the book (and who can tell what curiosities our own time will be found to have produced?) Barrett's book is both evangelical and catholic. The days of Watts's dominance have gone, and choirs and organs have replaced precentors and unaccompanied singing.

The preface of the *Congregational Hymnary* (1916) stated that it had retained nearly two-thirds of the previous book and that in making the new book the editors were guided by two principles, continuity and catholicity, bearing in mind the needs of 'a Communion embracing many shades of Christian piety and belief'. The editorial plan corresponds broadly with Barrett's. But hymns of the Trinity precede those of the individual Persons, while hymns of the Church precede those of the Christian life. There are fewer subdivisions in the missionary and national sections and the curiosities noted above have vanished. Missionary hymns and morning and evening hymns are included under the Church. There are even fewer Communion hymns (19, as opposed to Barrett's 22). But there are two new sections at the end: 45 hymns with refrains, reflecting the popular chorus-type songs associated with the Moody and Sankey revival, and a small number of Christian hymns and carols, supplementing those to be found earlier in the book with others which had also acquired popularity—a far cry from the days when the observance of Christmas was banned. The book ends with another extensive selection of pointed canticles, psalms and Scripture passages and of anthems. This probably represents the high point of the Free Church choral tradition, largely Anglican in inspiration.

Chants survive in *Congregational Praise* (begun in 1939 but not published till 1953), but anthems were published separately and never enjoyed the widespread use of their predecessors. The Trinitarian structure of the earlier books is retained, followed by *The Holy Scriptures* and *The Church*, with six sections: Its Fellowship; At Worship and Prayer; Baptism; The Lord's Supper; Militant on Earth (Home and Foreign Missions); Triumphant in Heaven (The Communion of Saints). *The Christian Life* is retitled *The Life of Discipleship* and has only eight sections (The Gospel Call; Response to the Gospel; Penitence and Forgiveness; Hope, Joy, Peace; Love to God; Consecration and Holiness; Faith and Aspiration; Pilgrimage and Conflict). The growing sense of the Church's engagement with the world and the lessening importance of nation and Empire are shown in the *Social and National* section under: The Love and Service of Man, The Nation and Peace and Brotherhood. *Times and Seasons* includes hymns for morning, evening, old and new year and the natural seasons, including harvest. *Special Occasions* embraces ordination, anniversaries and commemorations, hospitals and charities, marriage, funeral services and intercession. There is a special section for children, increasingly by this time present for the first fifteen minutes or so of Sunday morning worship, rather than in afternoon Sunday schools, and a rather larger selection of Christmas and Easter carols than in the *Congregational Hymnary*. A new section, *Metrical*

106

Psalms, surely owes its place to the growing relationship between the Congregational Union and the Prebyterian Church of England, culminating in the formation of the United Reformed Church in 1972. Another new section is *Congregational Anthems*, mostly fine hymns thought too difficult for congregations without a strong choral tradition, such as St Patrick's Breastplate and Baxter's 'Christ who knows all his sheep' in the settings by Stanford and Wood respectively. The final section before the Psalter is called *Chiefly for Private Devotion*, its hymns all in the first person. Although the decline of Free Church choirs was within sight, it is interesting to note that *Congregational Praise* adds to the pointed chants and psalms musical settings of the Ferial and Festal Responses and the Lord's Prayer.

At its formation the United Reformed Church decided to produce a supplement rather than a new main book, primarily because ex-Presbyterian congregations had only recently taken up *Church Hymnary: Third Edition*. It shared in the hopes for an intended ecumenical hymn book, though when these faded its members continued to sit on the editorial committee of *Hymns and Psalms*. In 1986 the General Assembly resolved to produce a new book. *Congregational Praise* was beginning to show its age, and the denomination was blessed with a large number of hymn writers. By this time the Reformed Association of the Churches of Christ had joined the United Reformed Church, bringing with it *The Christian Hymnary* of 1938, a book broadly similar in structure to recent Congregational ones, but, as befitted a Church which practised believers' baptism and a weekly celebration of the Lord's Supper, one which contained more extensive sacramental sections. The editorial committee was thus faced with the task not only of taking into account the three parent books of the uniting denominations but also the needs of those congregations in local unions with Methodists which might be using *Hymns and Psalms* or *With One Voice* (originally produced for the Uniting Church in Australia in 1977 but suitably amended for British use, 1979), the popularity of *Mission Praise* and the great variety of new words and music from new sources.

Over 2,000 unpublished texts alone were submitted to the committee, a sign of continuing creativity in hymn writing.

The new book, *Rejoice and Sing*, is structured theologically, and in a significantly different way from most of its predecessors. It begins with an Order for Worship, not of course prescribed, but indicating the greater acceptance of such forms in the Church. It continues with the Psalter and other ancient hymns and canticles, as well as short liturgical items like sung prayer responses, Kyries and one-line verses. The psalms are set in a variety of ways, some for chanting, but others following Gelineau and other musical traditions; and they are also set as in *Hymns and Psalms*, for responsive reading. The scheme itself is structured in the following way:

I. ONE GOD IN TRINITY

II. GOD'S CREATING AND REDEEMING LOVE
    A   God the Creator
- a. All God's Created Works
- b. Ruler and Guide of Creation
- c. God's Call to Righteousness
- d. God's Forgiving and Saving Love
- e. Praising the God of Creation

    B   God Incarnate
- a. Christ's Coming
- b. Christ's Advent
- c. Christ's Birth
- d. Christ's Epiphany
- e. Christ's Life and Ministry
- f. Christ's Passion
- g. Christ's Resurrection and Ascension
- h. Christ's Reign
- i. Praising the Crucified and Risen Lord

    C   God the Life-Giver
- a. The Coming of the Holy Spirit
- b. The Word and the Spirit
- c. Praising the Holy Spirit

III. CREATION'S RESPONSE TO GOD'S LOVE
    A   The Gospel
- a. The Need for God
- b. Hearing and Responding

B   The Church's Life and Witness
   a. Worship
   b. Baptism and Confirmation
   c. The Lord's Supper
   d. The People in God
   e. Growing in Faith
   f. Discipleship
   g. Pilgrimage
   h. Unity
   i. Proclaiming the Gospel
   j. The Continuing Hope
C   The Gospel in the World
   a. Christ for the World
   b. Love in Action
   c. Justice and Peace
   d. Healing and Reconciliation
D   ALL ONE IN GOD'S ETERNAL PRAISE

Among the significant changes, we may note the complete disappearance of the earlier triumphalist missionary hymns with their imperialist trappings. 'From Greenlands icy mountains' was apparently alive and well in 1953 but became impossible to sing not long thereafter, if only because the Churches planted in India and Africa had matured and were producing leaders and missionaries of their own. Many sang 'Hills of the north rejoice' lustily as schoolchildren, but in our age of mass media, rapid transport, international tourism and flourishing indigenous Churches, what sense can there be in evoking 'isles of the southern seas' as awaiting Christ or 'shores of the utmost west' (California?) as 'unvisited, unblest'?

The Church's theology of mission is understood rather differently now. While there rightly remain many hymns which look forward to the spreading of the Gospel throughout the world and to the coming of God's kingdom, there has been a great increase in the number of hymns on justice and peace, reflecting the theological shift away from a world view of the enlightened Christian West bringing religion and civilisation to heathen lands, towards one which stresses the Church's commitment to the kingdom of God and its values in all the strife and injustice of the world.

Solidarity with the oppressed, engagement in the struggle for human rights and dignity, and service of those in suffering and need are seen as important parts of the Church's vocation in the world. Hymns which take a world-denying view and seem to offer escape and a private sanctuary from the strains and stresses of life are less well represented, as in all main books since the last war, and especially those most marked by Victorian individualism. Nevertheless, some of the best survive: 'O Love that wilt not let me go' and 'Dear Lord and Father of mankind' make a different and equally valid contribution to the life of discipleship. But the Church is again discovering that it is not isolated from the world around. The heirs of those Congregationalists who sang Isaac Watts's beautiful Eucharistic hymn about the Church as 'a garden walled around' and 'a paradise of fruitful ground' in 'the world's wide wilderness' (a hymn full of allegorical interpretations of the Song of Songs going back to Philo and Origen) would not feel comfortable with such images now.

Other changes are connected to new approaches in worship. The decline in popularity of evening services means that evening hymns are less necessary than they were. Special occasions—marriage, funerals, harvest festivals—are seen more and more as part of a larger context, life in the family of God, or faithful living in God's world. Easter hymns and hymns of the communion of saints may be appropriate for Christian funerals, while harvest hymns have to be sung in the awareness of a hungry world. The Eucharistic section of the new book is richer than its predecessors, a sign of the growing convergence of Eucharistic theology between Catholic and Reformed Churches.

The apostolic classification of Christian praise into 'psalms and hymns and spiritual songs' has been pertinent throughout Church history. The Psalter has been used by Christians from the beginning, in direct translation, and from the Reformation in metrical paraphrase in the Western tradition. Hymns were originally liturgical anthems either on Old Testament models or specifically in celebration of the faith and its seasons of the year, for use in Office and Eucharist. In the Reformed and Methodist traditions they have developed into an essential element of the liturgy, offering freedom from the ping-pong of prescribed versicles and responses and making the proclamation a united and wholehearted act of the people. 'Spiritual songs' are of charismatic inspiration, or the result of particular experiences, the sufferings of groups despised and persecuted by the orthodox and established or of heart religion, whether with the psychological and doctrinal depth of Wesley or the ephemeral choruses of revivalism. The modern hymn book represents the evolution of all three and combines them, though sometimes uneasily and clumsily, together with a new category of hymns of social consciousness, which began with the Christian Socialists. Hymns are primarily to be sung as part of the worship of the people of God and this determines the arrangement of modern collections. By and large liturgy and society now predominate and personal religion may be less apparent than in the eighteenth and nineteenth centuries, except in the collections most influenced by neo-evangelism where personal experience may be most often celebrated in choruses and verses simpler if less profound and poetic than the hymns of the classical writers. The Reformed and especially Methodist custom of using the hymn book for private devotion seems to be ignored by the most recent compilers as it has been largely by those of the Church of England in the past. No book of the last twenty-five years is 'a little body of experimental and practical divinity' in Wesley's sense; which is not to deny that, used at home as well as in the congregation, a modern compilation may be of inestimable help in uniting private prayer to the liturgy and worship of the Holy Catholic Church.

NOTE

1   R. Tudur Jones, *Congregationalism in England*, London, Independent Press 1962. p. 299.

11

HYMN LECTIONARIES

Donald McIlhagga

'What hymns shall I choose for the service?' That is the question facing the leader of worship every week. Through the ages the Church has rarely prescribed the hymns to be sung on a particular Sunday or other Holy Days, even though it may have prescribed all the other parts of the service, so it may be expected that some time and care needs to be taken to ensure that the hymns are appropriate.

Sometimes one hymn has been prescribed. The ancient Office Hymns of the church come into this category. These Latin hymns were appointed for the hour services—*Iam lucis orto sidere* for Prime, *Nunc, Sancte, nobis, Spiritus* for Terce, *Rector potens, verax, Deus,* for Sext, and so on. They were omitted from *The Book of Common Prayer,* maybe for lack of English versions, but many have now been translated and can be found in some hymnals. *The English Hymnal* has the widest collection. 'Now that the daylight fills the skies' is fifth century, 'Come, Holy Ghost, with God the Son' is ascribed to St Ambrose (fourth century), as is 'O God of truth. O Lord of might', and 'O God, Creation's secret force' (for None), and probably most popular outside the *hours tradition,* 'Before the ending of the day' (for Compline) dating from the eighth century. There is a custom in some Anglican churches of singing such a hymn after the first lesson and before the Magnificat at Evensong. *The English Hymnal* has an index which extends the Office Hymn idea listing *Office Hymns for Saints' Days,* giving two or three hymns for 92 such days.

Other hymns have become very much associated with particular times or seasons or services. The metrical versions of some psalms have for long been associated with

The Lord's Supper in the Reformed tradition. Psalm 43, 3–5 'O send thy light forth and thy truth', used as an Introit and Psalm 24, 7–10 'Ye gates lift up your heads on high', used at the *Great Entrance*, were sung to elaborate tunes, *Invocation*, and *St George's, Edinburgh*.

Occasionally a particular hymn or type of hymn has been prescribed for a specific occasion. The Ordination Service in *The Book of Common Prayer* has 'Come, Holy Ghost, our souls inspire', or 'Come, Holy Ghost, eternal God'. Usually a hymn invoking the Holy Spirit is *required*, as in the Ordination of Elders in the United Reformed Church. Methodism of course has a Wesley hymn associated with its Covenant Service, 'Come, let us use the grace divine', adopted also by the Church of South India.

An extension both of the *Office Hymn* and of the *occasional hymn* has been made by Lutheranism. In addition to lections and psalms, a 'Hymn for the Week' is suggested. This is appropriate to the published theme for the day: thus, the First Sunday in Advent, whose theme is *The Coming Lord*, might have 'Lift up your heads, ye mighty gates'; or Rogate (Easter 5), 'Lord, teach us how to pray aright'. Such hymns relate to the lectionary in use before the Joint Liturgical Group produced *The Calendar and the Lectionary: A Reconsideration* in 1967.

In Anglicanism before this date the main helps available were tables of hymns, suggested first as an appendix to *The English Hymnal* (1933) and in a companion booklet to *Hymns Ancient and Modern Revised*. In *The English Hymnal* selections for Sundays and Holy Days included two hymns for Mattins, including an Office Hymn, two General hymns, (to be added at Mattins as required, or as alternates), a Procession hymn for certain days, one for the Litany, and four at Holy Communion—Before the Gospel, At the Offertory, At the Communion, and After the Blessing. Finally there are four for Evensong—an Office Hymn, one Instead of the Anthem, one Before the Sermon, and one After the Sermon.

The *Guide to the Use of the Revised Edition of Hymns Ancient and Modern* was produced to familiarise users with a *new* hymn book in an *average* parish. As with all such guides, its introduction points out that the selection is subject to the judgement of the incumbent who knows the devotional needs of his flock. Four hymns are provided for each of Mattins, Communion and Evensong. A Processional is suggested on certain festival occasions, and the hymns are given in the order they would normally be required in a service. Occasionally alternative hymns are also listed. The choice of hymns is often determined by some *feature* of the service, such as the Collect, the Epistle or the Gospel for the day. A separate list of Office Hymns is given for major feasts and it is suggested that the appropriate Office Hymn might be used before the service begins, or before the Psalms, or before the Magnificat. The hymns for Holy Communion are intended to be sung before the Our Father, after the Epistle, after the Nicene Creed or the Sermon, and after the Blessing.

An example of a recent Anglican book suggesting hymns for Sundays is *The New English Hymnal* which gives two lists for each day. The first for the Eucharist as the principal service follows the order Introit, after the Epistle, Offertory, Communion, Post-Communion. A Processional is suggested for major festivals which, if no procession takes place, might be substituted for the Introit. The introduction to this selection points out that the hymns usually follow the general theme of the lessons, though occasionally the link with a particular lesson is so clear that an alternative should be chosen if the lesson is not read in that year. The second list gives hymns as alternates to the first list or for a second service. This second list also contains hymns unrelated to any lectionary, enabling a congregation 'to enjoy a large and varied selection during the course of a year'. Certainly the enjoyment of the hymns themselves should be a factor in choice.

Prior to the 1967 Joint Liuturgical Group lectionary which was eventually largely adopted by all the mainstream Churches in Britain with the exception of the Roman Catholic Church, the other main selection of hymns was in *A Year's Praise* prepared by the Committee on Public Worship and Aids to Devotion of the Church of Scotland. It related to the Revised Church Hymnary. Three editions were produced, the last in 1959. There are lists for morning and evening including metrical psalms and paraphrases of scripture. The preface to the second edition says that 'some care has been taken to indicate, at the beginning and end of each list, items of praise really suitable for these positions, in which something familiar is generally desirable'. It is pointed out that the great festivals of the Christian Year 'gain in impressiveness' by the singing—in some form—of Te Deum, while Benedictus and Magnificat have an evangelical appeal of their own. It is suggested that these canticles may on occasion be substituted for the chanted psalm, there being two or more of these suggested for each Sunday or *special day*—Christmas, New Year, Epiphany, Candlemas, Mothering, Days in Holy Week, Ascension, Michaelmas, All Saints, Remembrance, St Andrew, Flower, Harvest, Assembly, etc. There are separate lists of hymns for Holy Communion—Pre-Communion, Admission, The Lords Supper itself (three sets plus Easter) and Thanksgiving after Communion. Finally there is a list of Anthems from the *Church Anthem Book* and *The Oxford Easy Anthem Book*.

In 1976 the Church of Scotland published *The Year's Praise* in succession to *A Year's Praise*, for use with *The Church Hymnary: Third Edition*, which had been published in 1973. Again two lists are produced for each Sunday, not however for morning and evening, but for two years, related to the two years of the JLG lectionary slightly modified. Six items are selected plus a children's hymn. One of the six is for times when Holy Communion is celebrated, and the other five for appropriate places in the service. Prose and metrical psalms are included. The selection makes provision for special days, though their number is somewhat reduced from its predecessor; it covers Christian Unity, Springtime, Harvest, Overseas, Remembrance, Christmas, Michaelmas, All Saints and, of course, St Andrew. Hymns for three series of services are suggested for Holy Week, the first thematic, the second on the events of the week and the third on the Seven words from the Cross.

There is an essential difference in the selections of hymns

made in the Anglican and Roman Catholic traditions on the one hand, and in the Reformed and Free Church traditions on the other. 'The hymn is for Free Church people a basic element in worship, in contradistinction to usage as an *Interlude piece* to break either a Quaker silence or an Anglican liturgy, either of which is complete in itself'. Most Free Church hymn books have a doctrinal schema, which becomes important as a book of personal devotion and a *teaching aid* as well as a vehicle for corporate praise. One book which has a 'liturgical scheme', and so is in itself an aid to choice for the order of hymns in worship is *The Church Hymnary: Third Edition*. Its three main parts are Approach to God, The Word of God: His Mighty Acts, and Response to the Word. Later smaller sections cover the Sacraments, Other Ordinances, Times and Seasons, Close of Service, and Personal Faith and Devotion. As the hymns for the beginning of worship come first and those for the end much later, it has been wittily suggested that churches using this book might have their hymn boards re-made in triangular shape! However, this arrangement of the hymns did not obviate the need for *The Year's Praise*.

The Year's Praise is the one selection which makes provision for the 'children's hymn'. This is becoming increasingly inappropriate for public worship if it is the kind of hymn written for children to sing alone. Worship is rightly seen as 'all-age worship' and hymns in more contemporary books, such as *Hymns and Psalms* and *Rejoice and Sing*, the book being prepared by the United Reformed Church, are those which can be sung by children and adults together. Such a hymn is often the second one sung before children engage in activities for their own age group.

The publication of the Joint Liturgical Group's work on the Calendar and Lectionary has helped to contribute to the spate of hymn-writing in recent years. Although *The Alternative Service Book 1980* of the Church of England played down the general themes of the Sundays, as indeed did the Joint Liturgical Group itself, in order to allow the biblical passages to 'speak for themselves', nevertheless these themes as well as the Bible passages have been used as a guide for hymn singing and they have certainly stimulated new hymn-writing. A good example is the previously neglected theme in the West, of the Baptism of Christ. It is still not easy to find good Epiphany hymns on this theme, but some now exist, like 'When Jesus came to Jordan' by F. Pratt Green. Some attempts have been made to do for the new lectionary what the Lutherans did for the old. C. G. Hambly has written a hymn for every theme, in *A Hymn for the Lectionary* (Caedmon Productions) and the Church of Scotland's *Hymns for a Day*, (1982) edited by Charles Robertson offers a song or hymn on the theme for each Sunday of the year.

Robin Leaver did a great deal of work to produce in 1980 *Hymns with the New Lectionary* (Grove Books). The next year a group in the York diocese produced *A Hymn Guide* (Mowbray). In 1983 the Epworth Press published *Companion to the Lectionary: Volume 2: Hymns and Anthems* by Alan Dunstan and Martin Ellis. This was the result of Anglicans and Methodists co-operating to list selections, in addition to Anthems, from four books, *The Methodist Hymn Book*, *Hymns and Psalms*, *Ancient and Modern Revised*, and *The English Hymnal*. Leaver pointed out in his Introduction, however, that 'the desire to locate hymnody suitable for the changing content of the Sunday lections has left no denomination behind. In America churches with a Presbyterian background are supplied with lists in a church music periodical (*Reformed Liturgy and Music* by Horace T. Allen), and The Chicago Diocese of the Episcopal Church issued its own supplement to the *1940 Hymnal* with an index for their three-year lectionary, and that here in this country Methodists include hymn selections in *Worship and Preaching* for Local Preachers and others and the Roman Catholics have been giving extensive listing since 1979 in the *Liturgical Music Planner*, where they make selections from 15 books, not only Roman Catholic'.

Leaver lists hymns from no fewer than 27 different hymn books in wide use. He followed certain principles of selection, namely: not every hymn under a particular theme is included, but normally only those available in a variety of books (though where a hymn is especially appropriate, even though it appears in only one source, it has not been excluded); not every allusion in a hymn has been taken up, for example, 'How sweet the name of Jesus sounds' is not included under the theme of *The Good Shepherd* simply because of the use of '*Shepherd*' in Newton's list of titles for Christ in verse 4; and third, no selection is made for the principal days of the Church's year, Christians, Easter, Pentecost as well as mid-week festivals such as Epiphany, Ash Wednesday and Holy Week where the problem is usually what to exclude rather than what to include.

The layout of each page of selections is clear—the day, the theme, the biblical references in the *ASB* lectionary (JLG slightly adapted) for the two years and two psalms as suggested by *ASB* (other books such as the *Methodist Service Book* and the *URC Service Book* have differing psalm selections at some points). Hymns are then listed alphabetically in a *grid* relevant to the Old Testament Reading, the Epistle, the Gospel, and the Psalm of the Day. Some hymns are simply on the theme without specific reference to the readings. There is a useful set of footnotes to record the major variations in text from book to book. Such footnotes make it possible to begin to appreciate the extent to which hymn book editors have attempted to '*improve*' original hymn texts. More recent books have in particular taken note of the current demand for inclusive language. In Leaver's selection not only the themes but the parts of the biblical passages which may not seem to refer to the theme have been allowed to suggest items, thus applying the JLG's view that the Bible be allowed to dictate its own conclusions. It is the Eucharistic lections rather than those for morning or evening prayer which have been determinative. A promise is made of a new hymn book under the title *Hymns for Worship* to fill the obvious gaps in the selection. This does not seem to have appeared. *Hymns and Psalms*, however, which was published in 1983, was compiled with the lectionary themes in mind. In its three sections of God's Nature, God's World and God's People it provides the widest selection yet published. Seven pages of *Liturgical Index* provide hymns on each theme, though not in a 'worship order', simply in the order in which they appear in the book.

Both Leaver and *Hymns and Psalms* have what most Companions to hymn books also have, an index of biblical passages and verses on which hymns are based, or which are alluded to in a particular hymn. These are extremely useful, though 43 pages in *Hymns and Psalms* is perhaps excessive and adds to an already bulky volume. The only other book offering selections on Sunday themes is the book which has modernised most of the hymn texts (though adding half a dozen of the best-loved traditional texts) *Hymns for Today's Church* (Hodder and Stoughton, 1982).

A Hymn Guide (Mowbray) was originally produced by a group in the diocese of York and has an Anglican bias. It does not however lay as much stress as Leaver on selecting for the Eucharist. It selects from 12 books, only one of which is from an ecumenical source, *With One Voice*, the British printing of the *Australian Hymn Book*. In addition to hymns on themes it has useful lists for Initiation Services, Gradual hymns, Offertory hymns and Post-Communion hymns.

Finally, the Epworth *Companion* must be noted. It offers a group of hymns from each of four books, plus anthems for all the lectionary themes, together with all the usual *extra* festivals, including Church Anniversary/Dedication, Education Sunday, Watchnight and the peculiarly Methodist Aldersgate Sunday to commemorate the Wesleys. Interestingly, the Methodist selections are all five hymns per service and the Anglicans four. This clearly relates to the comment above on the difference between the use of hymns in different traditions. The anthems are grouped in three lists according to technical difficulty. The introduction to the Choice of Hymns from the Anglican tradition makes the point that this selection is both more modest and more precise than that in either Leaver or *A Hymn Guide*. It is concerned with choosing hymns specially for the Eucharist and provides an Introit at the opening act of worship with the purpose of gathering the Congregation together, a Gradual designed to link the Epistle and Gospel (and so probably unsuitable if the Epistle is omitted), the Offertory intended to be suitable both at that point and also to the general theme of the day, and finally Post-Communion designed to be sung before the Blessing and Dismissal 'so that the strength of neither is weakened'.

The lists in this book, as in *The New English Hymnal* try to ensure a certain variety, of style, metre and mood, or key. Clearly there is nothing more deadening than having to sing (say) three eight-line hymns in one service, especially if they are all in a minor key! This however is only one of the dangers inherent in choosing hymns. Another exists because lists such as those referred to have been compiled. With the possible exception of *The Year's Praise* no attempt has been made to include all of the Hymnody available in any one book. The danger is that if only the lists are referred to many fine hymns will never be sung. The only solution is to get to know well the hymn book regularly in use and in addition as many others as is reasonable. Discover their treasures and note the variations in different editions of the one hymn. Look up a hymn book Companion to discover a hymn's origins and often the fascinating story associated with its writing or its subsequent use. And all this will add to the ability to choose appropriate hymns for the many different occasions on which the Church gathers for worship. If leaders of worship search the hymn book alongside searching the scriptures, then Sunday by Sunday and year by year the selection will always be creative and *fresh*.

Postscript

If real variety and appropriateness is to be achieved, not all the hymns wanted for every Sunday will be in the hymn book normally provided in a particular church. Apart from a decision to purchase a more up-to-date book, which many churches should consider, it may be expedient to resort to putting a duplicated sheet in people's hands, or using an overhead projector. In either case the copyright issues should not be ignored. Copyright details are usually indicated with the hymn or on a page of acknowledgements in a hymn book. Some hymns are out of copyright; authors and publishers may allow 'one-off' printing. It is always necessary, and indeed wise and courteous, to check. There are schemes whereby copyright on some contemporary material is covered by the payment of a fee to a central body.

BOOKS REFERRED TO

Hymns Books

Revised Church Hymnary, (Oxford)

Church Hymnary: Third Edition, (Oxford)

The Methodist Hymn Book, (MPH)

Hymns and Psalms, (MPH)

Hymns, Ancient and Modern, Revised, (Hymns Ancient and Modern Ltd)

The English Hymnal, (Oxford)

The New English Hymnal, (The Canterbury Press Norwich)

Hymns for Today's Church, (Hodder & Stoughton)

Hymns for A Day, (St Andrew Press)

Books and Booklets

The Testing of the Churches, Ed. R. Davies, (Epworth)

Book of Common Prayer, (Oxford)

A Year's Praise, (Oxford)

The Year's Praise, (St Andrew Press)

Hymns with the New Lectionary: R. Leaver, (Grove)

A Hymn Guide, (Mowbray/Cassell)

Companion to the Lectionary, Vol. 2 Hymns and Anthems: A. Dunstan and M. Ellis, (Epworth)

Guide to the Use of the Revised Edition, Hymns A. and M., (Hymns Ancient and Modern Ltd)

12

THE USE OF HYMNS IN THE CHURCHES

THE CHURCH OF ENGLAND

Donald Gray

Many of the average present day Church of England worshippers would be surprised, if not shocked, to discover
that the wide-spread acceptance of hymn singing was for
Anglicans no more than a mid-nineteenth century innova-
tion. They will probably not have realised that there is no
provision for the singing of hymns in the 1662 *Book of
Common Prayer* (with the sole exception of the two versions
of *Veni Creator Spiritus* in the Ordination of Priests and the
Consecration of Bishops). It was not until the passing of
The Act of Uniformity Amendment Act 1872 (36 and 36
Vict., C35) that they were officially recognised. Even then,
in the Judgement of the then Archbishop of Canterbury, E.
W. Benson, (*The Lincoln Judgement, 1890*) it was laid down
that, although it could be argued that hymns had received
authorisation from long standing custom, hymns should
not be inserted so as to interrupt the service.

  In the early part of the nineteenth century hymns were a
'party' matter. The early high churchmen (of the era before
the ritual controversies) were prone to describe hymn singing as an unacceptable 'protestant' activity which, because
of its observable popularity amongst non-conformists and
evangelical churchmen had no place in Anglican worship.
At that time many of the hymns had indeed originated from
those circles, for they quite naturally provided for the needs
of those who employed hymns in their worship. It would
only be later that the 'catholic' nature emerged of, say, the
Wesley hymns and the poems of such archetypal Anglicans

as George Herbert or Bishop Ken (who provided one of the finest hymns to celebrate the Assumption of Our Lady in 'Her Virgin eyes saw God incarnate born'). Meanwhile the works of Cowper, Newton and Montgomery seemed too tained with *enthusiasm* to suit the taste of the early Tractarians.

The first move away from Tractarian intransigence over hymnody came when, because of their considerable devotion to the study of the writings of the Early Christian Fathers, the Tractarians started to produce translations of the early Christian hymns, many of which had a long and honourable history in the Breviary.

1836 proved to be a year of intense activity. During that year Richard Mant, the Bishop of Down, Connor and Dromore, published a book whose contents weré clearly discernible from its title: *Ancient Hymns*. Meanwhile Isaac Williams, who had been the author of some of the Tracts which had given the Movement its name, had translated and published a series of hymns from the Parisian Breviary, and then in the same year John Chandler produced a book entitled *Hymns of the Primitive Church*. The developing years of the Oxford Movement produced many translations from the Greek and Latin. Some were the work of pioneers of the Movement such as Newman, Keble, Oakley and Caswell, and later, the prolific J. M. Neale.

Some original work in the field of hymnody began to appear from such unimpeachable Tractarian authors as Keble ('New every morning'; 'Sun of my soul'), Newman ('Praise to the holiest'; 'Lead kindly light'), and Faber ('My God, how wonderful thou art').

By mid-century any reserve among Anglo-Catholics about singing hymns had disappeared and the result of this was the first substantial collection of hymns for use in the Church of England. Considering the history of that development it is no surprise that the book, first published in 1861, was entitled *Hymns Ancient and Modern*. The book was the work of a redoubtable team whose members were all drawn from those who had been influenced by the Oxford Movement. The outcome at the time was a quite remarkable *volte-face* because many evangelical churches declined to use *Hymns Ancient and Modern* on the grounds of its high church provenance! Yet this particular hymn book would come to be regarded as an undoubted symbol of a middle-of-the-road, average, 'no extremes' Church of England parish. *Hymns Ancient and Modern* held the field for many years until two important books, which both adopted a high standard of musical content, appeared. *The English Hymnal*, published in 1906, was unashamedly 'catholic', while *Songs of Praise*, which appeared in 1926, was a product of twentieth century liberalism.

Since then these books, with the exception of *Songs of Praise*, have appeared in revised editions. *Hymns Ancient and Modern* has undergone this process twice; first *Ancient and Modern Revised* in 1950, and then, more recently, *Hymns Ancient and Modern New Standard* in 1983. This latest book incorporated two separately published supplements: *100 Hymns for Today* (1969) and *More Hymns for Today* (1980). *The English Hymnal Service Book* of 1962 was merely a condensation of the larger book. A supplement, *English Praise*, was produced in 1973, with *The New English Hymnal* coming out in 1986.

An entirely new book was *The Anglican Hymn Book* of 1965. This came from evangelical sources as did *Hymns for Today's Church* which appeared in 1982.

'Of the making of hymn books there is no end', a present-day Ecclesiastes might say. However, there is one book which will probably never be produced—an official Church of England hymn book.

* * *

THE CHURCH OF SCOTLAND

Colin R. Williamson

That hymns are a comparatively recent feature of Church of Scotland worship is to be explained by reference to the attitude of the Genevan reformers. In common with other reformers, Calvin rejoiced in the opportunity of restoring to the people their proper part in the Divine Service: 'It is a thing highly expedient for the edification of the church to sing some Psalms in the form of public prayers'. The Psalms in metre were for him the people's part in liturgy, prayers integral to the service.

Calvin's preface to the 1543 edition of *Marot's Psalter* shows why the line was drawn at psalms and the traditional canticles. Words sung in church must be holy and such as invite us to pray to God, praise him and meditate upon his works. But, as Augustine says, no one can sing worthily of God except he has received power from God. We can have no better than the psalms of David, words which God has put into our mouths that we might exalt him. As for music, Calvin believed that it should be simple with weight and majesty. He was strongly opposed to choral singing and to part harmony.

Prior to the Scottish reformation, a considerable Lutheran influence was at work. An important example of this was the production by three Dundee brothers, the Wedderburns, of *Ane Compendious Buik of Godlie Psalms and Spirtual Sangis*. Produced around 1542 and commonly called *The Gude and Godlie Ballatis*, this collection included hymns of Lutheran origin rendered into Scots along with such items as the 'Decalogue', 'Veni Creator', 'Song of Simeon', 'Song of the Blessed Virgin Mary', and 'Thanksgiving After Receiving the Lord's Supper'. *The Gude and Godlie Ballatis* was widely used in family settings and for religious instruction. For many years the hope was maintained that the collection might be revised for inclusion with the psalter but despite the commissioning of several people by the General Assembly, the work was never done and the *Ballatis* passed into history.

The development in the mid-eighteenth century was the movement towards approval of the Paraphrases (*Translations and Paraphrases in verse of Several Passages of Sacred Scripture*). This process, begun by the General Assembly of 1741, was dogged both by the delaying tactics of those who believed that only the psalms of David should be used in public worship and by the disturbance of normal life during and after the 1745 Jacobite Rising. At length, by an Act of 1781, the Assembly appointed 'these Translations

and Paraphrases to be transmitted to the several Presbyter-
ies of this Church, in order that they may report their
opinion concerning them to the ensuing General Assembly;
and in the meantime, they allow this collection of sacred
poems to be used in public worship in congregations where
the minister finds it for edification'. The ensuing General
Assembly heard nothing more about these paraphrases,
'arranged according to the order in which the several passages
of Scripture lie in the Bible, and a few hymns subjoined', and
while the permissive legislation which they enjoyed fell
something short of full formal approval, the paraphrases
became immediately popular and were widely used. In
party terms, the first 33 from the Old Testament pleased
Calvinists and moderate deists, whilst the new Evangelical
party welcomed the 34 New Testament paraphrases.
Writers of the paraphrases included Addison, Doddridge,
and Watts, as well as the Scots contributors, and selections
are to be found as hymns in contemporary hymn books.
The entire collection of 67 paraphrases and five hymns continues to be bound up with the *Scottish Psalter 1929*.

So far, all material used in worship could be said to be
scriptural, directly relating to biblical text. The dissenting
Churches led the break with the practice of 300 years. It was
the Relief Church, the most liberal of the Presbyterians,
which first produced a hymn book. A *Selection of Hymns
and Sacred Songs* was approved by that church in 1794.
Again on the liberal wing, the Seceders after the 1847 union
produced *The United Presbyterian Hymn Book* in 1851.
This collection was heavily indebted to Watts, Newton,
Wesley, and Keble.

In 1866 the Established Church produced its own book
which was improved and published in 1870 with 200 hymns
as *The Scottish Hymnal* and was intended 'for the use of
such congregations as may wish to avail themselves of it'.

The Free Church Assembly of 1872 approved its first
hymn book; enlarged, it appeared in 1881 as *The Free
Church Hymn Book*. Thus the three great churches of
divided presbyterianism, the Established Church, the Free
Church, and the United Presbyterian Church, each had its
hymn book, produced without co-operation. This typified

many aspects of church life in an age when one dissenting church would vie with the other as to whose spire would exceed the height of that on the parish church!

To some extent, the growing demand for hymns in every section of the divided church corresponded with a change from objectivity and intellectualism as Westminister Calvinism gave way to the subjectivism of the Evangelical party. Sankey's *Sacred Songs and Solos* was welcomed particularly in the new tenement parishes of urban expansion.

The production in 1898 of *The Church Hymnary*, authorised by the Church of Scotland, the Free Church of Scotland, and the United Presbyterian Church, (together with the Presbyterian Church in Ireland), was a significant reflection of changing attitudes as all three steered courses towards union.

The Free Church and the United Presbyterian Church united in 1900 and the resulting United Free Church was finally reunited with the Church of Scotland in 1929. Production of *The Church Hymnary: Revised Edition* had been a joint venture. It was published in 1927, and with the union, it was warmly received as a 'new book for a new church'.

In 1973, *The Church Hymnary: Third Edition* was published as 'a hymn-book for the use of the people of God in public worship'. The structure is based upon the Eucharistic Order of Public Worship, and the attempt was made to ensure that the words and not the tunes had priority of selection. Approaches were made to many traditions regarding the possibility of a combined book, but in the end only the Church of Scotland, the Presbyterian Church in Ireland, the Presbyterian Church of Wales, the United Free Church of Scotland, and the Presbyterian Church of England participated in the venture.

In today's Church of Scotland, few worshippers will be aware that hymn singing is a comparatively recent feature of the service. If much has been gained by the development, two ideals have been lost: first, the high place given to Scripture as the text of the people's prayers and praise; and second, the original intent that what is sung should be integral to the service, true liturgy.

THE BAPTIST TRADITION

Neville Clark

In the broad sense, Baptists are heirs of the Reformation. That at least means that they do not have some wholly independent story in terms of music in worship that is all their own. They belong within a stream which has fertilised many denominational soils and which has been partly driven by prevailing winds both theological and secular.

In a similar broad sense, Baptists have puritans for their forefathers. That also imposes a slightly narrower frame of understanding. We have probably outgrown the once popular caricature of the puritan spirit that dealt in labelling adjectives such as negative, restrictive, philistine. If puritan attitudes are to be rejected, they must first be understood, and that particularly in relation to beauty. Architecture may offer the clearest signpost and example. There are comparatively few early *puritan* meeting houses left standing in the land, but it would be perverse to claim that those which remain lack beauty. They are simple, they are plain, they are austere; they are seldom ugly. Music, of course, does not constitute an exact parallel in all respects. In architecture and building the reformation of the sixteenth and seventeenth centuries worked upon formed traditions that were themselves the product of rich development. There was much to inherit, to adapt, to rebaptise. Music, on the other hand, comes to full flower after the Reformation rather than before, certainly so far as congregational participation is concerned. Yet the basic parallel remains. In the formative years of the reformed traditions church music is designed to adorn worship and perhaps even to be enjoyed by its performers, but not to be listened to inactively or to be passively admired. Its beauty is in its honesty and simplicity.

It remains true that our puritan forbears tended to shun music in worship or to treat it with extreme suspicion. To that extent the popular caricature is not wholly divorced from the reality. Yet part of the reason lay in the fact that the apparently negative verdict was rendered by people who saw quite clearly and knew only too painfully what music could do, people who knew that it could sanctify disobedience and menace sacrificial living and corrupt at its heart the worship of God. The judgement implicitly being recorded was that music unredeemed and unbaptised may, by its sensuous beauty, set worshippers wallowing in emotional experience, set their souls soaring to heights of exaltation, and thereby stand between them and the God of righteousness who demands obedience and ensure that they never arrive even within hailing distance of the Cross of Jesus Christ.

Yet to speak of Baptists in their originating historical perspective is to narrow the frame of reference even further. It is to identify specific currents within the broad reformation and puritan streams. The most vigorous current is named *sola scriptura*. The subsidiary current is labelled antipathy to set forms. The first enthroned the necessity for precise and positive scriptural warrant for any worship practice. The second exalted maximum freedom in worship for the unfettered operation of the Spirit. Through the filter of the first the metrical psalms might just squeeze. By the standard of the second even the singing of metrical psalms stood condemned. The emerging composite authorisation was almost bound to stress heavily the charismatic qualifier 'be filled with the Spirit' which immediately preceded the 'psalms and hymns and spiritual songs' legitimated by the letter to the Ephesians. If all this seems meagre, it could be and was powerfully argued by Baptists rejoicing in a new if somewhat austere liturgical and spiritual springtime. It could be and was undergirded by a whole battery of supplemental reasoning which negated common musical *texts* and their corollary, unison singing, by reference to the presence at worship of women on the one hand and unbelievers on the other. And doubtless the contrary practices and presuppositions at home in opposing Christian traditions subconsciously fuelled hostility. In any event, as we move from the 'General' or arminian Baptists of the seventeenth century to the 'Particular' or calvinist Baptists of the closing decades of that century, a significant change is registered. Almost one hundred and fifty years before the Church of England in 1821 officially authorised the use of hymns in public worship, Benjamin Keach, minister of Horsley-down Baptist church in Southwark followed New Testament pattern in introducing the singing of a hymn at the close of the Lord's Supper. By 1697 Joseph Stennett had provided a collection of hymns for use at Communion. The camel's nose of modern hymnody was in the nonconformist liturgical tent. By the early eighteenth century even the General Baptists were beginning to capitulate. It must however be remembered that singing did not necessarily involve the use of instrumental music.

If Baptist worship during the late eighteenth century was affected by the Evangelical Revival and the outburst of praise and song it brought with it, the influence of the Oxford Movement of the Church of England was arguably and ultimately more significant. Much of importance to Baptist church life in the second half of the nineteenth century could be significantly plotted by way of mingled fascination with and reaction against the Tractarian legacy. In this curious and uneasy symbiosis, theological vitriol could find itself diluted by liturgical pretensions. Attitudes to music in worship did not escape unscathed. The splendid ceremonial, the solemn music, the concern for beauty, the rich devotion, were greeted with widespread revulsion. Yet they raised questions and, in an age of cultural advancement, could prompt strange echoes. Particularly in town and city, the choir and the organ were making an entrance, the oratorio and the anthem were making their bid for prominence, and John Wesley's stricture on 'the unseasonable and unmeaning impertinence of a voluntary on the organ' was no longer to be widely heard in the dissenting land. Chants and canticles were no longer totally foreign bodies in the Baptist bloodstream. They were mediated through the broader channels of Nonconformity.

A glance at the modern succession of Baptist hymnals tells something of the changing story. When in 1900 the *Baptist Church Hymnal* replaced *Psalms and Hymns* (1858) there was provided a supplement containing chants and anthems. There was to be no *revision* of it in 1933, as there was of the hymnal itself. Fresh grappling with material for what was somewhat optimistically described as 'congregational chanting' awaited the appearance in 1962 of the *Baptist Hymn Book*. It was indeed the hymnal of 1962 that revealed a belated musical lurch into the twentieth century. As Baptists were the last to be affected by the emphases of the Liturgical Movement, so they were among the last of the major denominations to give official expression in hymnody to the musical attitudes and standards associated with Vaughan Williams, Dearmer, and *The English Hymnal*. Ironically, by the time the *Baptist Hymn Book* appeared, the tides were already running in different directions. The Twentieth Century Church Light Music Group had tabled a quite different agenda for the future. The musical language of the dance hall was offering itself as the *lingua franca* of the liturgical world. The era of the loose-leaf, constantly revisable, religious song collection was in train. The Hymn Book of 1962 had caught the beginnings of the gentler of the winds of change by incorporating, though perhaps not too happily, two of Geoffrey Beaumont's syncopated tunes. In 1974, in an attempt to run with at least some of the loose balls, a supplementary collection of hymns *Praise for Today* involving 106 mainly twentieth century tunes was produced. A significant minority of them were hardly the stuff of which congregational praise is made. Current travail towards producing another new denominational hymnbook is inevitably beset with pressures and unsolved questions.

It is a far cry from the certainties of the seventeenth century to the confused contemporary Baptist landscape. Yet there are continuities; where there is change the reasons for it are not all shrouded in darkness; and even the ironies of history have something to tell us. From first to last, music has remained in a real sense incidental to corporate worship. Arguably, its ranking current functions are masking, backing, and mood creating. It covers entry, withdrawal, or necessary movement. It supports singing, it strikes a suitable note by assisting feeling tones. Nor is this surprising. For its originating traditions have always pressed Baptist worship in the direction of the declaratory and didactic mould. The Word of God is to be spoken and heard. Music is seldom too far away from other components of corporate worship in being viewed as an adjunct to the sermon; for worship is seen as essentially concerned with a receiving rather than with an offering, with divine approach rather than with human response, with Bach in addressing music to the congregation rather than with Palestrina in addressing music to God.

Of course, there are minority reports to be rendered. The nineteenth century emergence of the Baptist denomination as a self-confident mainline communion opened it to wider cultural and aesthetic currents within the national life. In the wake of the organ's dominance, music crept more towards centre stage, though ironically the entry into this inheritance was predominantly at the beginning of a century-long period beginning about 1860 that saw British organ building in rapid retreat from its erstwhile competent maturity, and when the decline was at last reversed in the 1950s the rumours of electric guitars and bongo drums were already bringing fear to the more staid of Baptist hearts. Ecumenical exposure and the cross-fertilisation it imposed speeded a new musical concern, of which the creation in 1962 of the Baptist Music Society was a significant, if not powerful, portent. Emphases characteristic of the Liturgical Movement rubbed off in corners of the denominational life. All these factors combined to foster a concern for music that was less peripheral and to sustain understandings of corporate worship that accorded to music a deeper significance at least in restricted circles.

There is, however, a further minority report to be tabled. Among the mainline denominations the Baptist probably has been of recent decades the most obvious stranger to the prevailing consensus of the hour and the last to be significantly touched by such consensus. The reasons for this are many and complex. The results of it have been crucial. It might be broadly true to categorise the last half-century in the following way. The 1930s and 1940s saw the rediscovery of the Church as part of the Gospel. The 1940s and 1950s saw the Liturgical Movement at full flood. The 1960s and 1970s saw the Charismatic Movement sending ripples in ever-widening circles. Because Baptists largely missed out on or came exceedingly late to the rediscovery of the

Church, their tentative and tardy domestication of the Liturgical Movement widely misinterpreted it in superficial fashion as though it was essentially concerned with fixity instead of freedom and reverent solemnity in place of informality. Because the sum and substance of the Liturgical Movement gained so little foothold, the seed of the Charismatic Movement encountered a soil ill-prepared healthily and soundly to contain it.

What has this to do with music in worship? Much, in every way. For the Charismatic Movement provided a significant spur to the flooding of worship with a type of vernacular tune of a different character from that of the classical hymn, and imposed it on a situation which had in general failed earlier to absorb insights about music, worship and the Church which might have proved counterbalancing and corrective. Familiar arguments about musical standards are important. Less familiar arguments about the understanding of the Gospel subtly communicated by musical forms are more important still. Yet, just at this point, two underlying assumptions need clearly to be exposed.

The one surfaces in the familiar question as to why the devil should be given exclusive rights to all the best tunes. If something is popular and effective, should it not be exploited? The argument is not automatically damned by pointing out that it sounds like a variation of the case for the end justifying the means. What may be required is a clearer and more explicit recognition that it depends on the assumption that the Gospel is unaffected by the channel of communication employed. All kinds of modern techniques and contemporary idioms may be validly employed because the Gospel is an insulated, timeless, verbally protected reality detached from any and every container. It is an explosive bullet totally immune in substance and impact from the gun that fires it and the casing that encloses it. If this assumption cannot finally be allowed to stand, then the argument becomes and must become an argument not finally about musical taste or musical standards but about fidelity to the Gospel. And then, if the rough verdict on the progression of congregational music in worship during this century is found to be one of 'from the sanctimonious, through the stark, to the secular', that judgment will be of theological rather than historical moment.

The second assumption is equally critical. If it be asked whether Baptist worship is viewed as a family or a public matter, a strong case could be made for the conclusion that it is in the former direction that the evidence increasingly signals. The point may scarcely need labouring. In all sorts of ways, Baptist churches, and not these alone, self-consciously act and behave as, in the best sense of the word, 'in-groups' with an intense family feeling and a warm communal life. This fact has widespread theological implications not least about the understanding of the church and its worship. It represents a position wholly in harmony with many of the pressures stemming from the Charismatic Movement. The strengths of the assumption undergirding it are obvious. The problem with assumptions is that they tend by definition to evade scrutiny.

The implications for music in Worship again are patent. There are certain things that are both proper and permissible within the family setting. The wider community may for certain key purposes be ignored. You may validly use in worship what to many outside the immediate family may be embarrassing, unintelligible, or just bad art. The problems start if the assumptions are challenged, if the Church is seen as a universal fellowship, if worship is seen as public worship offered to God and comprehending all sorts and conditions of men and women. For then the family may have at this point to consider renouncing some immediate pleasures and indulgences in the name of a wider responsibility and a deeper commitment to God and the Gospel.

Smooth and quick answers to the debate would be arrogant. What is crucial is that the debate is properly launched and that it takes place on the real issues. Those issues are not peculiar to Baptists. Whatever their resolution may finally be, Baptists are unlikely to deviate profoundly from their originating tradition, believing that beauty must always be subservient to something more central and important. Music, art and song find redemption as they mirror holiness and in some sense minister to it. If a choice has to be made, God must be worshipped in the beauty of holiness rather than the holiness of beauty.

* * *

METHODISM

A. Raymond George

'Methodism was born in song.' So began the Preface to *The Methodist Hymn Book* of 1933. John Wesley indeed published a hymn book as early as 1737, before the great spiritual experiences which changed the lives of him and his brother Charles at Whitsuntide 1738. Thereafter Charles wrote literally thousands of hymns, and John, who also wrote some hymns, published several hymn books, some of them with tunes. The definitive edition was the *Large Hymn Book* of 1780, 'A Collection of Hymns, for the use of the people called Methodists', often simply known as 'Wesley's Hymns', and described by him in the Preface as 'in effect, a little body of experimental and practical divinity'. As Methodists are often accused of overvaluing the Wesleyan hymns, let us cite a Congregationalist, Bernard Manning: 'This little book... ranks in Christian literature with the Psalms, the Book of Common Prayer, the Canon of the Mass'.[1] It is not, like most modern hymn books, arranged under the Persons of the Trinity or the seasons of the Christian year: it is, as Manning said, 'a spiritual biography of the sort of person whom he called in the 'Preface' a real Christian'.[2] The greater part of it consists of sections For Believers Rejoicing, Fighting, Praying.... and so on. There are also sections For the Society Meeting, Giving Thanks, Praying, Parting.

The reason for this is that though Wesley expected the people to attend the public worship of the Church of England, he intended his hymn book for the use of the Methodist societies, which held simple preaching-services at five in the morning and five in the evening. 'Some may say "Our own service is public worship". Yes in a sense: but not such as supersedes the Church Service. We never designed it should.'[3] Yet gradually the Methodists began to hold the Church Service in their own chapels, in London for instance, at West Street as early as 1743. Some of their earlier hymn books were no doubt used on such occasions. The service of Holy Communion could be enriched by *Hymns on the Lord's Supper*, by John and Charles Wesley, 1745; this contains a rich eucharistic theology which to this day has not been fully explored.

After Wesley's death there occurred a gradual separation from the Church of England and eventually the Methodists came everywhere to hold their morning service at the usual Church hour of about 10 or 11 am, and while in some places they used the Church Service, that is the *Prayer Book*, or our venerable father's abridgement, that is Wesley's *The Sunday Service* 1784, in most cases they used a service which was a kind of cross between a simple preaching-service and Morning Prayer. A similar form was used in the evening, for Methodism entirely abandoned Evening Prayer. The Communion Service was not held weekly, but monthly or quarterly, often after the evening service. To meet these and other requirements and to include hymns by other authors the Wesleyans added supplements to the 1780 hymn book, though some of the other branches into which the Methodists split produced hymn books of their own.

Eventually in 1904 the Wesleyans produced *The Methodist Hymn Book*, which was arranged in a more modern manner, and after Methodist Union in 1932 there emerged in 1933 a book bearing the same name. Fifty years later there was published *Hymns and Psalms: a Methodist and Ecumenical Hymn Book*, 1983, in the preparation of which members of other churches assisted.

There have been other books also, intended for Sunday Schools, or to supplement the Hymn Book, but the books listed above have been the main official books. While the use of the hymn book is not compulsory, the Methodist Conference authorises it just as, like most other churches, it authorises the service book; so that the hymn book, as in some other churches, has an official status. Methodism has spread to many parts of the world, and other Methodist Conferences mostly do the same, sometimes using the

British book, but often compiling books of their own, sometimes of course in other languages; some of Charles Wesley's hymns are translated and take their place among the hymns composed in the local language.

Correspondingly hymns have a unique place in the affection of the Methodist people, who, it is often said, learn their theology as much from the hymns of Charles Wesley as from the *Sermons* of John Wesley, though it is *Sermons*, together with the *Notes on the New Testament*, which constitute the official doctrinal standards. 'Hymns', said Bernard Manning, 'are for us Dissenters what the liturgy is for the Anglican. They are the framework, the setting, the conventional, the traditional part of divine service as we use it. They are, to adopt the language of the liturgiologists, the Dissenting Use. That is why we understand and love them as no one else does.'[4] Methodists have traditionally been reluctant to be called Dissenters, but they would gladly endorse this view, which affects the way the preacher (not the choirmaster) chooses the hymns to suit a particular service.

One way of doing this is to express certain aspects of worship through the hymns rather than through other forms. Thus for instance if a hymn is a metrical psalm or a scriptural paraphrase there is no need to read that passage of scripture; if a hymn is an adequate expression of, say, adoration of the Trinity or confession of sin, there is no need for that element of worship to be given further expression in the prayers. When the service had often a simple form, with perhaps only one lesson and one prayer in addition to the hymns and sermon, there was much to be said for that view. Such services, however, were based too much on the style of the five o'clock preaching services, and lacked something of the fullness of the Church Service, even though the hymns could do much to remedy the deficiency. To day it is more common for Methodist services to have a greater fullness, and in the *Methodist Service Book* of 1975 'The Sunday Service' has a shape and fullness similar to those of the Eucharists of other branches of the church, and 'The Sunday Service without the Lord's Supper', though it is what is sometimes technically called a *dry* service, also contains all the main elements of public worship.

Have hymns then become unnecessary in Methodism? Certainly not. The traditional form of the Eucharist, as well as having the unchanging prayers and the items often set to music such as *Kyrie, Gloria in Excelsis, Credo, Sanctus, Benedictus qui venit,* contains as 'proper' items, not only the collects and lessons but also certain other pieces such as the introit, gradual, alleluia (or other acclamation), and communion antiphon, which serve, as it were, to comment on and enrich the course of the liturgy. In the Roman rite these have mostly shrunk to a verse or so, though the recent reforms have expanded and emphasised the gradual. Metrical hymns are prescribed only in the divine office, apart from a few special occasions, such as some of the ceremonies of Holy Week. It is now, however, not uncommon in Roman churches for hymns to be sung at some of these points, usually in addition to the prescribed text. Methodists, however, nearly always sing a hymn at most of these traditional points, though they rarely sing the *Credo* and other such fixed parts of the liturgy with the occasional exception of *Gloria in Excelsis.* Thus 'The Sunday Service' suggests hymns at the following places: at the beginning of the service, as a possible alternative to 'Glory to God in the highest', before the Gospel, at the Setting of the Table, and just before the Blessing. No hymn is suggested at the Sharing of the Bread and Wine, but during the lengthy administration in the well-attended services of John Wesley's time the singing of hymns was common, and this practice has to some extent been revived in recent times as for example at Ordinations, when several hymns are sung at this place. At 'The Sunday Service without the Lord's Supper' the suggested points are at the beginning, between the opening prayers and the lessons, before the Gospel, after the Creed which follows the Sermon, and before the Dismissal. It is not fair to write off such services as 'hymn sandwiches'; they are full acts of worship, enriched with hymns.

It is sometimes said that the use of hymns is inferior to and less scriptural than the use of psalms which largely constitute the traditional introits and graduals. Sometimes in the Free Churches a psalm is read as a lesson, but *The Methodist Service Book* does not favour that method. In addition to a full complement of lessons (three for the morning, two for the evening), the book provides a psalm, or portion of a psalm for the morning and one for the evening of each Sunday or other special day. They are 'for optional use at any point in any service where a Psalm is required or desired'.[5] Moreover, the General Directions of *The Sunday Service* say: 'In place of a hymn, a psalm, or portion of a psalm, or canticle may be sung or said'.[6] *Hymns and Psalms* as its name implies, provides a selection of psalms and canticles, suitably pointed and provided in the appropriate edition with chants for this purpose, as did its predecessor. It is more customary, however, simply to read them responsively. Apart from the divine office, there is in any Western church some danger of the psalms being too little used, though the committee which prepared *Hymns and Psalms* was surprised by the vigorous and widespread public reaction arguing strongly and consistently for the inclusion of the psalms.[7] Very often, however, the suggested psalm is omitted; but some of the hymns are in fact metrical psalms, or paraphrases which, as Isaac Watts said, make David speak like a Christian; and many other hymns especially by Watts or the Wesleys, though not based on a psalm, are so full of scriptural allusions that they fit perfectly into the liturgy and make in a more extended way the same kind of 'comment' as is made by a gradual or other such item.

A further mark of the importance which Methodists attach to hymns is that at the Baptism of those who are able to answer for themselves, at Confirmation, at the Covenant Service and at Ordination appropriate hymns are not merely suggested but actually printed in the Service Book. Sometimes the words 'or some other hymn' are added, but this does not apply to 'Lord, in the strength of grace', one of the hymns at Confirmation, nor indeed to 'Come, Holy Ghost, our souls inspire ', one of the hymns at Ordination. This follows the example of the Prayer Book as regards Ordination, but the other cases are uniquely Methodist.

It is not common in Methodism for *Kyrie* (which does not occur in the Service Book), *Gloria in excelsis*, and so on, to be sung, though *Hymns and Psalms* contains a setting of

'Glory to God in the Highest' by Christopher Walker. In the very few churches where Morning Prayer is still in use, the psalms and canticles are usually sung to chants.

John Wesley greatly disliked anthems, but subsequently they came into use, at least in the larger churches, and an anthem is often sung in place of one of the hymns. Often a shorter piece is sung as an Introit before the first hymn.

Methodism very rarely has a *said* service like a Low Mass without hymns or the early Communion service of an Anglican Church. Even the simplest service, such as early Communion or a funeral service, or the daily prayers of a college or other residential community, will almost invariably include one or two hymns.

It is sometimes said that Charles Wesley's hymns strike a too subjective or personal note, and indeed it is a mark of Methodism to emphasise that faith must be personal. The Christian must be able to say, as John Wesley did on the 24th May 1738, that Christ 'has taken away *my* sins, even *mine*'. Yet most English-speaking Christians at the festivals and other seasons express the great objective truths of the faith in Charles Wesley's words: on Advent Sunday, 'Lo, he comes with clouds descending'; at Christmas, 'Hark! the herald-angels sing' (the hymn is Wesley's, though the first line has been altered); at Easter, 'Christ the Lord is risen today' (perhaps beginning at the verse 'Love's redeeming work is done'); at Ascension, 'Hail the day that sees him rise'. Such hymns contribute greatly to the tone and *feel* of those days.

Such an enrichment is always available. A service without hymns may in a sense contain all the essential parts of public worship, but wisely chosen hymns, some, but not all, by Charles Wesley, can make a kind of scriptural comment on each part of the service as it proceeds, and add immeasurably not only to the sense of congregational participation but to the whole tone of the service. Methodists, like other Christians, do not always live up to their principles or make the wisest use of their own treasures but they would say that the Wesley hymns and the Methodist way of using hymns in general are one of the greatest treasures which they can contribute to the universal Church.

NOTES—METHODISM

1 *The Hymns of Wesley and Watts*, London 1942, p. 14.
2 *Ibidem*. p. 11.
3 Minutes of Conference 1766.
4 *Op. cit*. pp. 133–4.
5 *The Methodist Service Book*. p. C2.
6 *Ibidem*. p. B2.
7 *Hymns and Psalms*. Preface.

* * *

THE UNITED REFORMED CHURCH

Donald McIlhagga

The United Reformed Church inherits the usage of English and Welsh Congregationalism, The Presbyterian Church of England, and The Churches of Christ. Hymnody has always been the main way that music has been used in the worship of the three traditions and now of the URC. Erik Routley, surely the URC's greatest hymnologist, called hymns 'delightful and dangerous things', and rightly claimed that for Free Churchmen they have always been inseparable from worship. They are part of our corporate response to God, and are perhaps the most memorable formulations of the Faith.

Both Congregationalism and Presbyterianism in England claimed the Puritans as their ancestors, and through them the inheritance of Calvin and Reformation metrical psalmody. Their books, however, have never included a complete psalter, but, rather as their selections have been seen, 'the cream'. In addition, there was the full 'Christianised' psalter of Isaac Watts on which to draw. What Wesley is to Methodist hymnody Watts is to Reformed, and he remains to this day the author with most texts in the books with widest use, with wonderfully rich hymns like 'When I survey the wondrous cross', and 'Jesus shall reign where'er the sun'.

For a long time Dr Watts's *Hymns and Psalms* was the

141

standard non-conformist hymn book. Its *Advertisement to Readers* of 1718 includes the instruction: 'Let the clerk read the whole psalm over aloud before he begins to parcel out the lines, that the people may have some notion of what they sing, and not be forced to drag on heavily through eight tedious syllables without any meaning, till the next line comes to give the sense of them.' Perhaps Reformed worship has always been too much of 'the head'? It took until 1833 for an annual meeting of the Congregational Union of England and Wales to ask for a supplement to Dr Watts, which was produced remarkably quickly—620 hymns published in 1836 as the *Congregational Hymn Book*, revised in 1844.

Along the way, there have been innumerable local books produced, and not least of these was by Watts's contemporary, Northampton's Philip Doddridge, whose Scripture paraphrases we still sing. The beginning of English Presbyterian hymnody must have been Suffolk Samuel Burry's *Psalms, Hymns and Spiritual Songs* of 1707, incorporating the texts of Richard Baxter. *The Complete Watts* finally disappeared with *The New Congregational Hymn Book* of 1858—with its 1000 items. A generation later in 1887 the *Congregational Church Hymnary* appeared, an attempt, as has been made by every generation since, to be contemporary whilst keeping the best of the old—a task entrusted to the famous Dr Barrett of Norwich. This was followed by *Congregational Hymnary* in 1916, with its second volume of Chants and Anthems. Finally, 1951 saw the publication of what indubitably proved to be the best of the series, *Congregational Praise*. The decision to compile it was taken in 1939 but the war prevented a start being made until 1944. It was compiled under K. L. Parry and Erik Routley with the strong musical influence of Eric Thiman. The contribution of the Scottish Metrical Psalter is reduced to sixteen portions, but there is an extensive section of prose psalms and canticles to add to the 700 or so hymns.

Although individual Presbyterians are to be found back to the mid-sixteenth century, and Congregations back to the mid-seventeenth, the Presbyterian Church of England was not formed until 1876. There had been considerable Scottish influence in one of the bodies which united to form that Church, but nevertheless it took a 'Free Church' position and severed links with the Church of Scotland. It produced its own *Church Praise* only six years after being founded. This was revised in 1907 and in addition to hymns included metrical psalms (74), prose psalms and canticles (43), anthems, and interestingly, arrangements of *Sanctus*, one with a full setting of *Sursum Corda*.

As has happened so often, then, a 'new' denomination felt the need to have its *own* book to help weld together its fellowship. This had been true of the *Congregational Hymn Book* and it was to be true of the URC supplement, *New Church Praise*. However when a generation later a new book was needed for Presbyterianism a 'tentative and provisional' collaboration began with those other Presbyterian Churches in Scotland and Ireland which had undertaken a revision of the 1898 *Church Hymnary*. The *Revised Church Hymnary* of 1927 was authorised by the General Assembly of the Presbyterian Church of England and is still in use today in some URC churches, not however with the full psalter as in Scotland, but with its own supplement of 57 metrical psalms and 52 prose psalms and canticles.

When the two Reformed traditions united in 1972, the *Church Hymnary: Third Edition*, in which the English Presbyterians were also involved, had been published only two years before and the time was not right for a new main hymn book. But the era of '*Supplements*' had come, and partly to help the URC to find its own identity, and partly because the URC had most of the contemporary hymn writers amongst its members, including Kaan, Gaunt, Wren, Routley, Micklem and Bayly, it produced *New Church Praise*. These men were all producing hymns to contemporise worship with texts about the city, about scientific discovery, industry, and modern life. In addition, the supplement recognised the strong growing trend which saw worship as 'all-age', so that hymns were needed, and were now supplied, not 'for children' but 'for children and adults to sing together'.

In 1982 the Re-formed Association of The Churches of Christ was unified with The United Reformed Church and brought with them *The Christian Hymnary* which had been compiled in 1938. Their tradition of Believers' Baptism and Weekly Eucharist was to add to the richness of the Union and some of their hymn writers like Tickle and Robinson were to offer valuable additions to URC worship. The eighties also saw a 'diversifying' of interest in some URC churches into charismatic hymnody represented by *Mission Praise* and other books, and into ecumenical usage represented by the Australian hymn book entitled in Britain *With One Voice*, adopted by many united Methodist— United Reformed churches.

All these books, together with *Hymns and Psalms* recently produced for The Methodist Church by an ecumenical group, were the standard reference books from which the URC began in 1986 to select hymns for a new main hymn book to be published in 1991 under the title *Rejoice and Sing*. It aims to produce not only the 'best selection' of hymns for our day, but also what it believes to be the 'best versions' of those hymns. A great deal of work has been done on a reselection of verses, re-translation of ancient texts and texts written in other languages, and on the updating of texts where words or phrases have become archaic. It can be claimed that this hymn book will be the first truly 'inclusive language' hymn book that has fully respected the original texts of authors both old and new.

* * *

ROMAN CATHOLIC TRADITION

Edward Matthews

The Background

One of the causes of the Reformation was the impossibility of full participation in the liturgy by the laity. The use of the Latin language and the consequent reservation to the clergy of active involvement in the liturgy were a scandal to the leaders of the reform. This lack of popular lay involvement extended to music used in worship; choirs, or scholas, existed and monastic communities maintained a vigorous music tradition, but the laity had no real part in them. Liturgical music at the beginning of the sixteenth century was, in general, confined to the specialist performer.

This situation had prevailed for many centuries. The Roman Stational Mass of the seventh century, destined to have a profound influence on the liturgy of the West, knew nothing of popular participation by song. Music there was in plenty, but performed by trained cantors and scholas. Nevertheless, though the laity were silent, their prayerful enjoyment of the liturgy was enhanced by listening to these trained experts. As the Middle Ages progressed, musical forms developed, became more complicated, and therefore rendered popular participation more difficult still. The need for trained groups of singers must have meant that only well-endowed, centrally located churches and monastic communities could rejoice in the luxury of liturgical music.

Religious song was not entirely absent from the lives of the laity, however. Carols, originally associated with secular dances, took on a religious character, and the growth of popular, non-liturgical devotions in the thirteenth and fourteenth centuries involved popular song. But by the time of the Reformation, liturgical music was confined to relatively few churches and performed by their specially trained choirs.

Post-Reformation

The Council of Trent (1545–1563) was Rome's answer to Reform. It had much to say about the theology and discipline of the Sacraments, but left most of the ritual details to be worked out by subsequent commissions. It had intended to deal with the reform of liturgical music during the Council; not surprisingly this too was put off. Gregory XIII, in 1577, attempted a revision of the music for the main chants of the Mass, but this also was abandoned. In 1614, however, an edition was published with papal approval, but it came to be regarded as something of a desecration of the old Gregorian chant.

The political and religious situation in the British Isles

effectively suppressed the musical celebration of the Roman liturgy for the best part of three centuries. Fortunately, William Byrd (died 1623), a Catholic, was allowed to continue his work and he composed much fine music for the Latin liturgy. How much, if any, was performed during this period is doubtful; it demanded musical resources which the recusant Church was unable to muster.

On the European continent, meanwhile, a totally different situation prevailed. The reforms of Trent had put a stop to any kind of natural liturgical development, but this had little or no effect upon music, and the centuries following the Council witnessed a musical flowering in the liturgy which still today is one of the riches of Western culture. From Palestrina (died 1594), through Mozart (1791) and on to Gounod (1893), a succession of Catholics composed for the liturgy. Papal, episcopal, and princely chapels sustained and promoted some of the best composers and musicians of the times.

Beautiful and enduring as it was, such music was rarely liturgical in the proper sense. Although the music was a glorification of God, it was more of a performance, allowed of no participation by the majority of worshippers, and rarely touched the general run of the Catholic Church where choirs and choristers and orchestras were almost unknown. The style of music, too, owed more to the opera house than to the inner meaning of the liturgy. In many instances, the liturgy simply provided a convenient setting for a concert performance.

An interesting exception to this practice arose in Germany during the eighteenth century. In parts of that country there had remained a practice of singing the congregational parts of the Mass according to the old Gregorian chant. Building on this, as it were (though not without some opposition), there grew the practice of singing parts of the Mass in the vernacular. While this essentially popular and congregational singing was taking place, the priest recited or even sang in Latin the same parts of the Mass. This continued in some parts down to modern, pre-Vatican II times.

About 1840, there began a movement destined to have a

profound influence upon the music of the Catholic Church in Britain, as well as the rest of the world. Dom Prosper Gueranger, Abbot of Solesmes, initiated a movement for the restoration of the ancient Gregorian chant, its notation and its performance. Dom Prosper had in view the full participation of the entire congregation—an aim not easily attainable by parishes lacking the skills and resources of monastic communities.

The Abbey of Solesmes continued the work of its initiator and, from an official point of view, this reached a climax in November 1903 with the publication of a *Motu Proprio* by Pope Pius X on Sacred Music. Some of the principles laid down by the Pope were perhaps a reaction to the excesses of the Baroque period and after. But they were, above all, an affirmation of the work of Solesmes and the first hints of what was to come, almost exactly sixty years later, in Vatican II's Constitution on the Sacred Liturgy. In his introductory section Pius X states that he wishes to see restored the true Christian spirit which can be acquired 'from its foremost and indispensable fount, which is the active participation in the holy mysteries and in the public and solemn prayer of the Church'.

In 1903, the generality of Roman Catholics in the West regarded the read, or recited, Mass as the standard form of worship. Pius X took a new direction by stressing the fact that sacred music was an integral part of the solemn liturgy. He went further by specifying the nature of that music:

'... Gregorian chant... is... the chant proper to the Catholic Church.... The Gregorian chant has always been regarded as the supreme model for sacred music so that the following rule may be safely laid down: The more closely a composition for church approaches in its movement, inspiration and savour the Gregorian form, the more sacred and liturgical it is; and the more out of harmony it is with that supreme model, the less worthy it is of the temple. The ancient traditional Gregorian chant must, therefore, be largely restored in the functions of public worship...'[1]

The Roman Catholic Church in Britain was not slow to act upon the Pope's injunctions. Gregorian chant, or plainsong as it was often known, quickly gained a foothold in the churches and religious communities. *Plainsong for Schools* eventually became familiar to many Catholic boys and girls, at least to those lucky enough to gain entry to Catholic grammar schools, or to private schools conducted by monks or nuns. The parishes, too, felt the influence of the melodies restored by the monks of Solesmes. Many a congregation was quite able to sing in unison the *Missa de Angelis*, or a chant version of the Creed. Undoubtedly this was a step forward in community participation in the Church's liturgy. It was, however, limited.

Trained choirs were still needed to sing the chants of the Proper, or variable, parts of the Mass. Furthermore, the priest was still required to recite quietly those parts already being sung by choir or congregation. Music, despite the words of Pius X, was still not regarded as integral to the liturgical celebration; or, to put it another way, the participation of the laity was not fully *valid* unless repeated by the priest.

The re-birth of Gregorian chant did not exclude other forms of liturgical music. Polyphonic settings of the Mass were still sung. A few city-centre churches could afford to maintain semi-professional choirs. Other churches with less talent attempted some of the great choral settings, but the results were often less than pleasing. Today, many Roman Catholics look back on those days with more imagination than accuracy.

Apart from the Mass and the Divine Office (sung in very few places), there was another level of worship known as 'popular devotions'. The most well-known was *Benediction of the Blessed Sacrament* which the more devout might attend a couple of times each week. Rosary, Sermon and Benediction was especially well-attended on Sunday evenings before the introduction of the evening Mass. Mid-week devotions to the Virgin Mary, or another saint, were also popular. At various times of the year, such as the *Feast of Corpus Christi*, processions and pilgrimages figured large in the lives of the Roman Catholics. Although Gregorian chant and polyphony were not unknown in all these examples of popular devotions, there was nevertheless a musical culture quite distinct from that prevailing at Mass or the Divine Office.

This music was for community participation and, for the most part, in the vernacular. It was largely made up of hymns, although litanies (most in Latin) played a part too. For many Catholics this was in fact the only regular religious musical form and it therefore occupied an important place in their devotional lives. 'Soul of my Saviour'; 'Hail, Queen of Heaven'; 'Sweet heart of Jesus'; 'Lord for tomorrow and its needs' will remain firmly fixed in the emotions of many a Roman Catholic long after the memory of Gregorian chant has faded.

The flavour of these hymns is often Italian, and some of the most popular words were written by Frederick William Faber (died 1863), an Oratorian who espoused a more fervent and demonstrative form of spirituality. Another Oratorian, Edward Caswall, (died 1878), also contributed to the growth of popular hymnody which perhaps was rather late in flowering because the preceding centuries of repression had prevented all but the most basic forms of worship.

Immediately prior to the Second Vatican Council (1962–1965) music was not regarded by British Roman Catholics as integral to the celebration of the liturgy. While particular choirs attained high levels of competence and popular devotions attracted a sizeable number of participants, it has to be said that the majority of worshippers either rarely attended any service which included music, or were required to be silent listeners when they did.

Vatican II and today

Significantly, the first document to be promulgated from the Council was the *Constitution on the Sacred Liturgy* (4 December 1963). Its principal aim can be summed up in its own words: 'In the restoration and promotion of the sacred liturgy the full and active participation by all the people is the aim to be considered above all else, for it is the primary and indispensable source from which the faithful are to derive the true Christian spirit.'[2] These words derive directly from those of Pius X, sixty years before. And it is this statement which is the context within which the Church's present attitude to music in the liturgy must be understood.

Chapter VI of the Constitution is entirely devoted to sacred music. Gregorian chant is accorded pride of place, the pipe organ held in high esteem, but, equally, other forms of music and instruments are allowed, even encouraged, as long as the active participation of the people can be promoted.

Four years later (5 March 1967) a more detailed document *Musicam Sacram*, was published in Rome. Since its publication this has embodied the Roman Church's thinking on the place of music in the liturgy. (A new document is awaited at the time of writing). Paragraph 5 amply summarises its spirit and ideas:

'Liturgical worship is given a more noble form when it is celebrated in song, with the ministers of each degree fulfilling their ministry, and the people participating in it.

Indeed, through this form, prayer is expressed in a more attractive way, the mystery of the liturgy, with its hierarchical and community nature, is more openly shown, the unity of hearts is more profoundly achieved by the union of voices, minds are more easily raised to heavenly things by the beauty of the sacred rites, and the whole celebration more clearly prefigures that heavenly liturgy which is enacted in the holy city of Jerusalem.'

Once more, we have an echo of the words of Pius X, but the situation is now rather different because of the detailed nature of the reforms carried out in the Church's liturgy and, above all, because of the widespread introduction of the vernacular language in place of Latin.

Musicam Sacram stresses that music is not merely an embellishment of the liturgy, but is an integral part of it. Indeed, much of the liturgy, of its very nature, demands that it be sung. Processional chants, acclamations, psalms are some examples. Furthermore, the type of music employed must respect the meaning of the text and the nature of the particular celebration; a joyful round on Good Friday would be as out of place as a dirge at a wedding.

It is not expected that all that can be sung will in fact be sung at each and every occasion. The degree of solemnity of the celebration as well as the musical competence of the worshippers must be taken into account. With the Eucharist especially in mind, the Roman document lists the musical priorities according to their degree of importance. In the first degree are the opening greeting of the priest and the people's reply; the opening prayer; the Gospel acclamations; the prayer over the offerings; the Preface, its Dialogue and Sanctus; the Doxology of the Eucharistic Prayer; the Lord's Prayer and Embolism; the greeting of peace; the prayer after Communion; the formulas of Dismissal. In the second degree are the songs at the Entrance and Communion processions; the song after the first reading; the Alleluia before the Gospel; the Offertory song; the readings, if suitable. In Britain, there has been some re-arrangement of these priorities so that, in general, collects and readings are not sung and the priest-people Dialogue is more often recited.

This list gives some idea of the rich diversity of music which is necessary for a more ample celebration of the Roman liturgy; (and it should not be forgotten that we have here not touched upon the other sacraments, the Divine Office and other liturgies).

At the time of the publication of *Musicam Sacram* (1967) the Church in Britain did not possess the resources which would immediately fulfil the requirements of that document. Little suitable vernacular music existed and even the Latin liturgy in its renewed state was musically incomplete. (This has now been rectified with the publication of the *Graxdale*). From the beginning a few composers set to work, for example, Laurence Bevenot, Gregory Murray, Wilfrid Trotman, to provide suitable liturgical settings. However, far more commonly, there quickly grew the practice of singing hymns at the Entrance, the Offertory, Communion and after the Blessing—known as the 'four-hymn-sandwich'.

The hymns selected were at first those familiar to Catholics from the popular devotions. With remarkable speed, however, compositions from other Christian traditions were introduced—traditions more accustomed to vernacular worship. The overall result has been an enrichment of Roman hymnody: many Catholic hymns, inadequate both musically and textually, have fallen by the wayside and others have entered the repertoire, serving as a sort of ecumenical bridge. Examples of *adopted* hymns are, 'All creatures of our God and King', 'He who would valiant be', 'For all the saints', 'Ye choirs of new Jerusalem', and many others. Unfortunately, in too many communities, the four-hymn-sandwich has endured. What at one time was intended as a stop-gap solution has become the standard form of musical celebration.

Undoubtedly this situation has been prolonged by a lack of liturgical formation within local communities. At the same time, it has received some encouragement from the introduction of *folk music* and music originating in the charismatic movement. Many Roman Catholics in Britain now regard the Folk Mass as the typical form of the vernacular liturgy. Not a few parishes have two music groups, or choirs; one which sings folk music, and one which celebrates in the traditional Latin manner.

For the most part, the folk idiom is hymnodic. Even where the official liturgical texts are sung this is often done in the style of a hymn so that a single repeatable melody is utilised for totally differing parts of the liturgy, thus offending against one of the basic principles laid down by *Musicam Sacram* and, indeed, against the true meaning of the liturgy itself. While this is regrettable, it must be said that this form of music has contributed to a greater degree of community participation. It has led many communities to an understanding of the nature of liturgical celebration and it has filled a gap created by the rapid introduction of the liturgical renewal and the reluctance of some composers to meet the new needs of the Church.

Choirs, though nowadays far fewer in number, still flourish. The rich diversity of traditional music can be heard in many parish churches and cathedrals, often interspersed with modern vernacular pieces. Many choirs have adjusted well to the dual role of choral music and of supporting and sustaining congregational singing.

Formation, or re-education, remains a priority and will do so for a long time to come. To assist in this, the former Music Department of the National Liturgical Commission of England and Wales produced *Music in the Parish Mass* (CTS 1981), a companion volume to *The Parish Mass* (CTS 1981) and *The Parish Church* (CTS 1984). This is a succinct statement of the principles governing liturgical music, a description of the various roles, or ministries, in music, and practical guidelines for composers. Like its companion volumes, it has received the full approval of the Bishops' Conference of England and Wales and is therefore an expression of the bishops' policy regarding music in the liturgy.

Moving to the future

Now that the dust of immediate reform has settled, composers imbued with the spirit of the liturgy are coming forward with music of quality which challenges congregations to raise their sights—for instance, Geoffrey Bouton-Smith, Philip Duffy, Paul Inwood, Christopher Walker, Bernadette Farrell, David Saint, Ernest Sands. The actual text of the liturgy is being taken seriously so that, in the words of one musician, we are learning not to sing at Mass but to sing the Mass. Such an approach amply fulfils the Church's desire that music be regarded as a ministry. That is, that music be seen as an integral part of the liturgy, yet at the service of the liturgy.

Summing up, it can be confidently asserted that a musical revolution has taken place in the Roman Catholic Church in Britain during the past twenty years. Certain aspects of it leave much to be desired, but the overall result is one of definite gain. The full, active participation by the entire liturgical assembly, by the whole people of God, is being established as the Roman and normative practice. A hitherto silent congregation has taken possession of the liturgy—has been possessed by the liturgy—and has thereby constituted a more active, participating Church. The life and prayer of the Church has been immeasurably enriched.

NOTES

1   *Motu Propris Tra le sollecitudine.* Paragraph 3.
2   No. 14.

APPENDIX

THE CHURCHES' HYMN BOOKS

Charles Robertson

Some Churches formally authorise specific hymn books for use in public worship; others leave the matter open, so that the choice of hymn book lies with the local congregation, district, or diocese—or incumbent! But even in those Churches where there is an *official* hymn book, there may be no bar to other hymn books being used.

In addition, there is an enormous variety of hymn books available, and the use made of this range of hymn books varies even among congregations of the same denomination and in the same locality.

In these circumstances, it is impossible to be precise about the hymn books in current use in the Churches. All that can be done is to give a list of books that are known to be more or less widely used in each of the Churches, with the name of the present publisher and the date of publication where known.

THE CHURCH OF ENGLAND

1 **Hymns Ancient and Modern Standard Edition** 1924 Hymns Ancient and Modern Ltd

2 **Hymns Ancient and Modern Revised** 1950 Hymns Ancient and Modern Ltd

3 **100 Hymns for Today** 1969 Hymns Ancient and Modern Ltd

4 **More Hymns for Today** 1980 Hymns Ancient and Modern Ltd
(These last two were intended as Supplements to *Hymns Ancient and Modern Revised*; and were later bound together in one book, **Hymns for Today** 1983)

154

5   **Hymns Ancient and Modern New Standard** 1983 Hymns Ancient and Modern Ltd
(Contains all of *100 Hymns for Today* and *More Hymns for Today*, together with a selection from *Hymns Ancient and Modern Revised*)

6   **The English Hymnal** 1933 Oxford University Press

7   **The English Hymnal Service Book** 1962 Oxford University Press
(Selection of *The English Hymnal* with supplement of 36 items, mostly carols)

8   **English Praise** 1975 Oxford University Press
(Supplement to *The English Hymnal*)

9   **The New English Hymnal** 1986 The Canterbury Press Norwich, a wholly owned subsidiary of Hymns Ancient and Modern Ltd
(400 of the 656 hymns of *The English Hymnal*, plus 100)

10 **Songs of Praise** 1926 Oxford University Press

11 **The BBC Hymn Book** 1951 Oxford University Press

12 **Broadcast Praise** 1981 Oxford University Press
(Supplement to *The BBC Hymn Book*)
(These last two bound in one book in 1982, **The Broadcast Hymn Book** Oxford University Press)

13 **Anglican Hymn Book** 1965 Church Book Room Press Ltd

14 **Anglican Praise** 1987

15 **Hymns for Today's Church** 1982 Hodder & Stoughton

16 **With One Voice** 1979 Collins

17 **Hymns and Psalms** 1983 Methodist Publishing House

THE CHURCH OF SCOTLAND

1   **The Scottish Psalter** 1929 Oxford University Press

2   **The Church Hymnary Revised Edition** 1927 Oxford University Press

   The Church Hymnary: Third Edition 1973 Oxford University Press

3 **Songs for the Seventies** 1972 Galliard
   (A collection of 52 contemporary hymns)

4 **Hymns for a Day** 1982 Saint Andrew Press
   (A song or hymn for each Sunday of the year, related to
   the Lectionary in *The Book of Common Order 1979*
   drawn from *The Calendar and Lectionary* of the Joint
   Liturgical Group)

5 **Songs of God's People** 1988 Oxford University Press
   (Supplement to *The Church Hymnary: Third Edition*)

(Note: 1–5 above have *some* kind of official status)

6 **Sounds of Living Water and Fresh Sounds** 1977 Hodder
   and Stoughton

7 **Mission Praise** 1983 Marshall, Morgan, and Scott

8 **Songs and Hymns of Fellowship** 1985 Kingsway Publications

THE BAPTIST UNION OF GREAT BRITAIN AND IRELAND

1 **The Baptist Hymn Book** 1962 Psalms and Hymn Trust
   (777 hymns, with selection of psalms, canticles, and other
   Scripture passages for alternate reading or congregational chanting)

2 **Praise for today** 1974 Psalms and Hymns Trust
   (104 contemporary items, drawing upon wider than
   British resources)

3 **Baptist Hymns and Worship** (provisional title)
   (to be published in 1990)

METHODISM

1 **The Methodist Hymn Book** 1904 Novello and Company

2 **The Methodist Hymn Book** 1933 Novello and Company

3 **Hymns and Psalms** 1983 Methodist Publishing House

UNITED REFORMED CHURCH

1 **Congregational Hymnary** 1916

2 **Congregational Praise** 1951 Independent Press

3 **The Church Hymnary Revised Edition** 1927 Oxford
   University Press

4 **The Church Hymnary: Third Edition** 1973 Oxford University Press

5 **Christian Hymnary**

6 **New Church Praise** 1975 Saint Andrew Press
(Supplement to both *Congregational Praise* and *The Church Hymnary: Third Edition*)

7 **Rejoice and Sing** 1990

THE ROMAN CATHOLIC CHURCH

1 **The Westminster Hymnal** 1912 Burns and Oates

2 **The Parish Hymn Book** 1968 Cary and Co Ltd

3 **New Catholic Hymnal** 1971 Faber Music Ltd

4 **Praise the Lord** 1972 Geoffrey Chapman

5 **Celebration Hymnal** 1976 Mayhew-McCrimmon

6 **Songs of the Spirit** 1978 Kevin Mayhew Publishers

7 **More Songs of the Spirit** 1981 Kevin Mayhew Publishers

8 **Hymns Old and New** 1983 Kevin Mayhew Ltd

9 **Music for the Mass** 1986 Geoffrey Chapman
(Not a hymn book, but contains contemporary material for congregational singing)

Also published by
The Canterbury Press Norwich

THE WORD IN SEASON
Essays by Members of the Joint Liturgical Group
on the use of the Bible in liturgy
Edited by DONALD GRAY

This is a contribution to current exploratory work on the possibilities of an international ecumenical lectionary. The JLG's own calendar and lectionary made an important contribution to the revised service book in many churches. Here the Group looks again at the principles involved in the ordered use of the Scriptures in worship. '... an interesting collection of essays on sundry aspects of the Bible in worship'—Kenneth Stevenson, in *Expository Times*

216 × 135 mm   *148 pp. paperback*
ISBN 1 85311 001 9